"Darrell Gurney's book, *Headhunters Revealed!*, is a must read for anyone considering a job change or for organizations using search firms. It removes critical myths regarding the staffing industry."

— DAVID HARDER, PRESIDENT, CAREER MOTION, INC.,
AUTHOR OF *THE TRUTH ABOUT WORK*

"This book will undoubtedly help professionals learn how to advance and leverage their careers by working with 'headhunters.' Accurate, easy to read, and loaded with valuable information . . . you've got a winner here!"

— MIKE KAPPEL, PRESIDENT, TOP ECHELON NETWORK

"This book should be read and its contents thoroughly digested by anyone truly interested in managing their careers—or entering the placement and search industry! Packed full of useful information, tips, and techniques, I can honestly say, after twenty-eight years in this business, this book is the best I have read on the subject of job change and working with 'headhunters.' A must read."

— TERRY PETRA, CPC, CIPC, TOP SEARCH INDUSTRY
TRAINER AND CONSULTANT, AND CHAIRMAN OF THE
NATIONAL ASSOCIATION OF PERSONNEL SERVICES (NAPS)

"The author shows step by step how to use recruiters for your own benefit. As a college student, I recommend to everyone who wants to get ahead—read it! This book is your guide to the future."

— ANGELICA HUANG, ENTRY-LEVEL COLLEGE GRAD

"Darrell's expansive knowledge of the job search arena enables m to reach both the novice and experienced job seeker. The amples and illustrations are 'on target' with accepted career rategies. This book is a must read for unhappily employed and unemployed professionals at all levels."

— RD PARDUE, FORTUNE 500 HR DIRECTOR, AND
R VICE PRESIDENT/MANAGING DIRECTOR OF
MANAGEMENT CONSULTANTS

"I thought the material was very timely and practical. I would be thrilled if every candidate read this book before calling me or sending in a resume."

— LORA LEA MOCK, PRESIDENT, PROFESSIONAL
RECRUITERS, INC., AND CHAIRPERSON OF NATIONAL
PERSONNEL ASSOCIATES (NPA)

"In the increasingly maddening labyrinth of searching for the right career—a maze of job banks, web postings, and e-cruiters—the best source may still be the headhunter. Gurney explains the perspective, as well as the process, of the headhunter, lending some humanity to a much misunderstood profession."

— DANNY CAHILL, TOP SEARCH INDUSTRY TRAINER AND
RECRUITER, CAREER MANAGEMENT GURU, AND
PRESIDENT OF HOBSON ASSOCIATES

"Straight forward style makes it a fast, enjoyable read with great practical advice."

— KATHY SIMMONS, PRESIDENT, NETSHARE, INC.

"Informative, helpful, and offers the insight as to how the industry operates in today's world of computers and e-mail. I read it twice to make certain I did not skip or jump over material that was important."

— JEFF BEATTY, VP MARKETING-LEVEL JOB-SEEKER

"I would recommend this book for anyone searching for the right recruiter. More importantly, I would recommend this book for any recruiter searching for the right methodology. Perhaps we've found the best tool of all for bringing new consultants 'up to speed.' Since staffing is truly about helping people find the right career path, this book fills that niche nicely."

— ROBERT LENTHART, DIRECTOR OF TRAINING &
DEVELOPMENT, ACSYS, INC.

"*Headhunters Revealed!* is a street-wise book that shows how anyone can easily use the incredible leverage of representation by a recruiter to supercharge their career!"

> — Jeffrey G. Allen, JD, CPC, America's Leading
> Placement Attorney

"I liked the informal tone. I think that potential job-hunters could learn a lot from reading what you've written."

> — Pat Loomis,
> Executive Assistant-Level Job-Seeker

"Over the past 25 years I've read a number of books on headhunters. Darrell Gurney's *Headhunters Revealed!* made understanding the role of the headhunter and how to use a headhunter simple . . . something most other texts didn't do. I'd recommend including *Headhunters Revealed!* in the career resource center of any system responsible for helping people find their next job."

> — Dick Gaither, President, Job Search Training
> Systems, Inc., and author of *Wizard of Work . . .*
> *88 Pages To Your Next Job*

"If you're in the under-$100K bracket, this breezy little book is for you, because it concentrates on the contingency recruiters who fill most of these jobs. Arm yourself with the answers to questions the recruiter may ask. Never again will you have to go naked into a face-to-face or telephone interview."

> — James Kennedy, Founder, Kennedy Information,
> Inc., publisher of *The Directory of Executive*
> *Recruiters*

"Conversational writing style and sense of humor make for an easy and informative read for people wanting to work more closely with their recruiter."

> — Bob Mikesell, Partner, First Interview
> Network

"In an era when job-changers face an overabundance of less-than-satisfactory methods for advancing their careers, *Headhunters Revealed!* offers an insightful analysis of the ever-growing profession of search and recruiting and helps unlock the mysteries of how they can successfully utilize 'headhunters' to benefit from their unparalleled expertise."

— PAUL HAWKINSON, PUBLISHER/EDITOR,
THE FORDYCE LETTER

"If both candidates and recruiters read and used this book, it would go a long way to establishing a relationship built on mutual trust and expectations."

— BILL VICK, FOUNDER, RECRUITERS ONLINE NETWORK
(RON)

"Finally someone bridged the gap—the gap of understanding between the job seeker and the professional headhunter. *Headhunters Revealed!* is a valuable tool and should be added to your home business/personal development library. You will use it during your next employment search."

— AL SCHIRMACHER, CPC, PRESIDENT,
CAREER COUNSELING & SEARCH

"An honest approach to how headhunters work and what an applicant should expect. I appreciated your candid style."

— GARY HERMAN,
SALES MANAGEMENT-LEVEL JOB-SEEKER

"Loaded with valuable information for job seekers and professional recruiters alike. In an era where impersonal Internet job sites are becoming more common, Darrell correctly illustrates that anyone seeking a career change is still best served by an experienced, professional recruiter. I plan on using this book in our national training program."

— MIKE ETTORE, VICE PRESIDENT OF LEADERSHIP
DEVELOPMENT, KFORCE.COM

"FINALLY, someone has taken the mystery out of what headhunters do and made them accessible and easily understood in this very readable tome chucked full of practical, REAL advice on how to get a headhunter to notice you and work with you. This is required reading for any candidate who wants to develop a partnership with a recruiter, and any recruiter who is focused on lasting candidate relationships. I know I will recommend it to every candidate who contacts me."

— JEFF SKRENTNY, CPC, CTS, TOP SEARCH INDUSTRY TRAINER AND CONSULTANT, AND PRESIDENT OF THE JEFFERSON GROUP

"I would recommend Darrell's approach to anyone in the process of a job search. A *must read* book for anyone looking for that right job and how to find it."

— JOHN MCNAMARA, PRESIDENT, MCNAMARA & ASSOCIATES, AND FORMER FORTUNE 50 HR DIRECTOR

"This is great stuff! Finally, someone who knows what he is talking about has written an honest, insightful and completely useful guidebook for dealing with our industry!"

— JAMES R. GETTYS, PRESIDENT, INTERNATIONAL STAFFING CONSULTANTS, INC.

"Well-organized and detailed. It covers all facets of job search through recruiters."

— RUSS RIENDEAU, PARTNER, THOMAS LYLE & CO., AND AUTHOR OF *THINKING ON YOUR SEAT*

"Today, it isn't just about finding a job, it is about developing and managing a career. I would recommend this book to anyone who is truly serious about taking control of their work life and their future. It is a tremendous vehicle for delivering valuable career resources in a simple, yet powerful manner."

— CHERYL MCCLURE, DIRECTOR OF MARKETING, ACSYS, INC.

"Any candidate that is preparing to discuss their career and market their skills will benefit from reading your book."

— JIM SULLIVAN, PRESIDENT,
GALAXY MANAGEMENT GROUP

"This is a blueprint for getting the most mileage out of working with a headhunter."

— DAVE CALHOUN, PRESIDENT, SELECTIVE RECRUITING ASSOCIATES, INC.

"It is clear that you have a passion for writing, a passion for educating, and a passion for humor. I sat back, read it, and enjoyed!"

— VIKKI LOVING, PRESIDENT, INTERSOURCE, LTD.

HEADHUNTERS
REVEALED!

*Career Secrets for Choosing
and Using Professional Recruiters*

HEADHUNTERS

REVEALED!

Career Secrets for Choosing and Using Professional Recruiters

Darrell W. Gurney, CPC

Hunter Arts Publishing
Los Angeles

Headhunters Revealed!
Career Secrets for Choosing & Using Professional Recruiters
By Darrell W. Gurney, CPC

This book is available at a special discount when ordered in
bulk quantities from the publisher. For information, please contact:
Special Sales Department
Hunter Arts Publishing
P.O. Box 66578
Los Angeles, CA, 90066
or call (310) 821-6303

Grateful acknowledgement is made for: permission to reprint quotes from *Sharkproof* by New York Times #1 bestselling author Harvey Mackay, author of *Swim With The Sharks Without Being Eaten Alive*; quotes from THE ULTIMATE BOOK OF BUSINESS QUOTATIONS Copyright © 1998 Stuart Crainer, reprinted by permission of AMACOM, a division of American Management Association International, New York, NY, all rights reserved (http://www.amanet.org.)

This book is designed to provide accurate and authoritative information in regard to the subject matter covered. It is sold with the understanding that the publisher is not engaged in rendering professional career services. If expert assistance is required, the service of the appropriate professional should be sought.

The author and publisher have made every effort to ensure the accuracy and completeness of information contained in this book, yet *there may be* errors, inaccuracies, omissions, or inconsistencies herein. Any slights of people or organizations are unintentional. All resume examples are fictitious compilations from the thousands received by the author and are not meant to resemble any actual persons. The purpose of this book is to educate and entertain. The author and Hunter Arts Publishing shall have neither liability nor responsibility to any person or entity with respect to any loss or damage caused, or alleged to be caused, directly or indirectly by the information contained herein. If you do not wish to be bound by this, you may return this book to the publisher for a full refund.

Publisher's Cataloging-in-Publication
(Provided by Quality Books, Inc.)

Gurney, Darrell W.
    Headhunters revealed! : career secrets for choosing and using professional recruiters / Darrell W. Gurney — 1st ed.
    p. cm.
    Includes index.
    LCCN: 99-90916
    ISBN: 0-9674229-0-6
    1. Executive search firms. 2. Executives—Recruiting. 3. Career development.
I. Title.

HF5549.5.R44G87   2000   658.407'111
                                                  QBI00–250

To my own Hunter for life,
my son.

" . . . Enjoy your achievements as well as your plans.
Keep interested in your own career, however humble;
it is real possession in the changing fortunes of time.
Exercise caution in your business affairs; for
the world is full of trickery. But let this not blind you
to what virtue there is; many persons strive for high ideals;
and everywhere life is full of heroism . . . "

EXCERPT FROM *DESIDERATA*, FOUND IN
OLD ST. PAUL'S CHURCH DATED 1694

Table of Contents

PART III   USING A RECRUITER:

Putting Your Head to Work

PART IV   HI-TECH HEADHUNTING:

Resumes for Database Jungle Fighting

FOREWORD

Darrell Gurney has written a terrific Every Person's What's-Happening-Now guide to fast-forwarding your career through the use of professional third-party recruiters, more cozily called "headhunters." Gurney takes you inside the corridors of power in the recruiting industry, illuminating a world made murky by misunderstandings of the true nature of these career makers and breakers.

If ever there was a time in American history to grab onto professionals who can help you move up not one step at a time, but a flight of steps at a single bound, it's right now in this heady, dizzying seller's job market.

The headhunters described in this work fall into the category called contingency—or pay-for-performance professionals. This means that unlike retained headhunters who are paid whether they deliver results or not, contingency hunters don't get paid until you get hired. That incentive's a comforting thought, especially when you're on the early-to-middle upside of your career, struggling to rise to your personal zenith. You want somebody out there hustling hard in business moves that benefit you. A contingency headhunter can be that somebody.

The Century of Opportunity

Assuredly, the United States economy will cool at some unforeseeable point and jobs won't be as plentiful as they are today. And certainly, a number of jobs will migrate overseas in a relentless global march. But the smiley face for today's job seekers is found in definitive demographics: the first wave of the baby boomer generation will soon enter retirement years and the following generation X is pint-sized compared to its predecessor. This translates to an availability of more boss jobs with fewer competitors than we've seen in recent years, even when a thinning of management ranks is taken into account.

By reading this book, you confirm that you want your share of rewards in what futurists describe as the Century of Opportunity, business mavens characterize as the New Economy, and the recruitment industry sees as the Wild New Workforce compelling companies to go to extraordinary lengths to find the best employees. A headhunter can be your shepherd/near-agent/bodyguard and all-around career booster.

Your New Best Friends

Never forget that a recruiter is always—repeat, always—the client's person, first and foremost. After all, the client pays the bills.

But in a tight labor market, which is likely to be the case throughout this decade, the law of supply and demand takes over and the value of topflighter candidates rises sky high. While only a few years ago headhunters sometimes viewed even talented job seekers as coals in New Castle, today they're gold bars in Ft. Knox.

So the trick is to attract the right headhunters' attention and strategically position yourself in those recruiters' databases. Yes, databases—not filing cabinets. Although "paper" still works, especially at the most senior management levels, clearly, as a magazine cover proclaimed, The Internet Won. E-life is changing all of us.

As you enter Third Millennium job search, you'll need to expand your communications technology prowess, as well as update your understanding of recruiter-client-candidate relationships. And you'll need to know lots of nitty-gritty techniques and technology conventions that are evolving as I set down these words. Darrell Gurney—who clearly practices Third Millennium headhunting—does a very good job of showing you how to avoid the disappointment of being a Gutenberg candidate in a digital world. I think you'll find this book to be extremely valuable. I did.

— Joyce Lain Kennedy
San Diego, California

Careers columnist, *Los Angeles Times Syndicate*
Author: *Resumes for Dummies, Cover Letters for Dummies,* and *Job Interviews for Dummies.*

INTRODUCTION

headhunter, *n.* One who seeks out, decapitates, and preserves the heads of enemies as trophies. *Business.* A messenger of opportunity for career transition: see also *Your Ticket Out—and Up!*

This book didn't start out as a book. It began as a few informative pages about working with recruiters that I planned to add to my Web site. However, when delving, pen in hand, into everything job-seeking professionals should know about the mind and "mechanics" of executive recruiters, I found myself buried in notes. Finding no comparable source of information on the market for the average professional, my calling to spread the word grew beyond the Web site into what became this book.

The purpose is to empower you, the working professional, to reap every bit of potential career support from the executive search profession—and to protect and enhance your self-esteem in the process. Securing your right livelihood is an intimate activity of paramount importance, and it is easy to take everything *personally*. However, getting the most out of a headhunter means knowing how to manage that relationship *professionally*. To date, headhunting has not been a well understood profession in our society. With the significant rise in stature of the search industry over the last 50 years, most of today's professionals have interfaced with a headhunter in one way or another: some have contacted a recruiter for assistance, some have been recruited, and some have been "placed"—often more than once! But there is little awareness in the professional community of how to milk this free service for all it's worth—not just for a quick job, but for long-term career management. Beyond a brief, passing connection with a recruiter at some point in their career, professionals don't seem to know exactly what headhunters do, why they do it, or how the profession can best serve the job seeker. Yet such understanding can drastically impact success with recruiters—and, therefore, a successful career.

Headhunters aren't understood because, generally, they don't explain their work—they're too busy closing the next placement! Yet, if you, the career-minded professional, can step behind the scenes and climb into the headhunter's head, your discoveries will lead to lifetime career benefits. This book is your ticket!

Now and throughout the book, I'll state clearly: a headhunter can't place everyone. The search profession is not a social service—it is a client-company directed, money motivated business. Unfortunately, some less marketable candidates are not helped. Statistics show that only 10-15% of the candidates hooking up with search firms actually land a position that way. Although this seems a small percentage, consider that hundreds of thousands of professionals are placed by recruiters every year. Undoubtedly it is a viable avenue for career transition. Perhaps the 10-15% success figure could be increased by a more informed job seeker, a better educated candidate. Knowing how to choose the best headhunter for you, being aware of the most efficient and effective modes of submitting your resume, and understanding the long-term career potential of a "partner" in your employment corner are all factors that can increase your odds of success with a recruiter.

Here's an insider's perspective of the business of placing you in business. I hold nothing back—no trade secrets, no hidden agendas. As a matter of fact, some of my colleagues weren't all that happy with everything I revealed! They still entertain the notion that there is some "control factor" to be maintained with candidates by keeping certain things quiet. However, my purpose is to give it to you straight in order to foster more open, sound partnerships between career-changing professionals and those in the recruiting business. The idea is this: when you know how headhunters operate, their work will not only make sense, but you'll join them at the controls —for your *own* best interests.

HAPPY HUNTING!

DARRELL W. GURNEY, CPC

Grammar & Language Footnote

You'll realize in reading this book that I write as I relate to people—in a simple, down-to-earth manner, spiced with clever (and corny!) humor. Due to this relaxed style, I've always cringed at the supposed necessity to incorporate belabored, "politically correct" pronouns (e.g., he/she, he or she) into one's writing while, at the same time, felt that using the standard "masculine disclaimer" was inappropriate. I alternate gender-specific pronouns, but often use "they," "them," or "their" to refer to a single antecedent—such as, "A key factor in partnering with *a* recruiter is whether or not *they* take the time to listen to your needs and desires." It makes sense—plus, it's a darn sight simpler!

Another item: throughout the material, I often refer to executive search professionals as "recruiters." This term does not include in-house hiring agents of corporations, often operating as an adjunct of Human Resources under the title "Corporate Recruiters." The worlds of the in-house and search-firm recruiter are very different, and each adheres to its own unique conventions. A headhunter, you'll learn, is committed to getting you the best deal possible, whereas a Corporate Recruiter focuses exclusively on the company's interests. This exposé reveals only the world of the independent search professional, whether called recruiter or headhunter (or some other choice names). And, by the way, *headhunter* is *not* a dirty word! It is a badge worn proudly by practitioners of a vital professional service. One should be so lucky—and flattered—to have their head "hunted."

ACKNOWLEDGEMENTS

I put this off until the very end because, not only were people still showing up to help, but attempting to justly thank everyone involved was simply ominous. There are those who helped at all levels, and no input or support was too small. Though in no way all-encompassing . . .

First, I thank the friends, associates, colleagues, candidates, and other professionals who took time to review and comment on the initial manuscript. Nobody has time for these things, yet all found a way: Jeff Beatty, Gary Herman, Dave Bachman, Joan Friedlander, Brian Seastrom, Bill Goldberg, Joel Mottinger, Angelica Huang, Pat Loomis, John McNamara, Tony Causey, Carrie Bokar, Caitlin Welsh, Vince O'Neal, Russ Riendeau, Ray Spadaro, Leslie Gaber, Sandy Gorelick, Jim Tower, Bob Mikesell, Dave Calhoun, and Jim Gettys. Particular thanks are due those colleagues who stepped in early with words of encouragement as well as invaluable critiques: Al Schirmacher, Lora Lea Mock, Vikki Loving, and Bill Vick.

I thank the professionals in the trade who helped bring this idea for a book to fruition. For inspiration, I thank Mark Victor Hansen. For mentoring in the area of publishing and promotion, I thank Dan Poynter, truly the Dean of Publishing. They say behind every good writer is a good Editor, and I agree. I was blessed to have 2 great ones fall into my lap: Fred Sleezer, who began our relationship as a professional job seeker and turned Headhunter (don't ask me!); and Jane Schoenberg, without whose seasoned experience, warmth, and part-of-the-family friendliness I would have suffered a dreary process. For printing and design, I thank Barry Kerrigan, who helped out with experienced advice and ideas long before he was officially signed on. Laura Berton's cover photography, along with her fun and friendship, is also much appreciated. I gratefully acknowledge Joyce Lain Kennedy for her immediate and most gracious backing.

I thank Barnes & Noble for a writing place, Susan Shelton for noticing that I could write, my parents and family for a start in life, my friends who support my growth, my son who gives everything purpose, and God for Grace.

PART I

CANDIDATE BASIC TRAINING

A Hunting We Will Go . . .

Utilizing the free services of a professional recruiter, and using them responsibly, is one of the best career decisions you can make. There are certain undeniable benefits in using recruiters when you decide to make a job change. In more than 14 years of headhunting, I have interacted with individuals who say they "always find [their] own positions" or are used to "doing it on their own." Though this may be a valid attitude toward job change for some, especially prevalent with today's emphasis on the Internet, I believe it to be limited and that teamwork and partnership create far better results. Transitioning professionals, armed with a knowledge and understanding of the search industry, will find recruiters immensely valuable as a supportive avenue of career movement. For this reason, it is worth mentioning exactly *what* is to be gained from associating with headhunters and *why* they exist.

CHAPTER 1

Why Recruiters Exist and What They Do

There once was a firm named We're Growing
They grew sod and sold seeds for sowing
But with growing so fast
The staff just wouldn't last
Without help, no clients would be mowing!

The bosses were simply too busy
To find more good help made them dizzy
So they put out the word
Which a special friend heard
Who came quickly, stopping the tizzy

Her name, you might guess—Hedda Hunter
She helped out when things went asunder
Finding just the right folks
Who were freed from past yokes
To make WeGro Wall Street's hot number

They say now the grass is much greener
Than back when the staff was much leaner
Corporate clout they do wield
With the best in the field
Now on board to make the firm keener

As We're Growing arose from rancor
The owners and staff saw their bankers
To cash in the windfall
That Hedda brought to all
By spurring their growth—all do thank her

Obviously, for any industry to thrive as the recruiting industry has, there must be a significant demand for its product. Without going into a lengthy, historical account of the rise of employment services, let's simply note that, in some form or another, they have been around for the better part of this century. Professional-oriented *search* firms, or *headhunters*, as opposed to industrial labor or administrative agencies, have become significant players in the employment world since WWII. With the technology- and information- "ages" upon them, corporations have found it necessary to have outside recruiters fill their needs.

Of course, the services of professional recruiters are, like anything else, subject to the laws of supply and demand: when the economy is strong, headhunters are utilized more heavily than when it's weak. Yet, with the drift toward in-house Human Resource (HR) departments becoming more administrative in nature (payroll and benefits *administration*, worker's compensation *administration*, employee relations, etc.), there has been a growing trend in these departments to out-source their recruiting function regardless of the state of the economy. Other functional departments have followed HR's lead: if it's an Accounting department, they must focus on accounting; Sales on selling; Engineering needs to be engineering—none of these is geared for recruiting and resumes. Thus, the growth of outside recruiters.

For those who don't know exactly how the search industry operates, a basic description of its relation to HR and other hiring departments may help. As mentioned above, most HR departments, though initially created to oversee hiring and firing within corporate structures, have become much more administrative. They remain involved in terminations, due to potential legal liability, yet their ability to handle all aspects of hiring is quite limited. God bless them, but by the time all their other departmental duties are completed, there is little time left for anything else. HR is, essentially, an overhead department: it generates little that can be seen on the bottom line and, yet, costs a great deal to run. Therefore, there is rarely sufficient staff in HR departments to deal with all of the legally mandated functions, much less to handle every aspect of new employee recruitment. A company may run ads in newspapers or on the Internet, but often doesn't have the manpower to address and respond to those ads promptly. ENTER: The Recruiter!

AS THE HEAD TURNS

Hedda's Office: Scene 1/Take 1

A C T I O N !

HEDDA HUNTER: "Professional Search. May I help you?"

HENRY ROLLINS JOSEPH ("H.R. JOE"): "I hope so. I'm calling from Big Universal Services Year-round (B.U.S.Y.) Company. We are looking to expand a great deal this year and would like to discuss your recruitment services."

HEDDA HUNTER: "Great! Well, I'd love to get to know more about your company to see where we can be of service. Tell me what you do."

H.R. JOE: "Well, mainly we stay busy, and we consult other companies on how to stay busy. Our philosophy here at B.U.S.Y. is that busy-ness is good business. We employ about 1,200 experienced busy professionals now—we call them 'B.U.S.Y. Ps'—and we want to expand our

beginner consulting ranks by another 50 this
year—we call them 'B.U.S.Y. Bs.' We have
specific requirements that must be met for
someone to be employed by B.U.S.Y. That is
why we are coming to you. Not just anybody is
a B.U.S.Y. body."

HEDDA HUNTER: "I see. Well it sounds, how should I say, very . . .
industrious! Um . . . Have you taken any steps
thus far to find candidates to fill your 'B.U.S.Y. B'
positions?"

H.R. JOE: "Yes, well, we did run a full paper ad in the Big
City Times . . . "

HEDDA HUNTER: "You mean a full *page* ad."

H.R. JOE: "No, a full *paper* ad. Only problem is that now
we have so many resumes cluttering our offices
that we had to hire another consulting firm,
Directional Intelligence Guides (D.I.G.), to help
us find our desks."

— **C U T !** —

The crux of what the recruiter offers is a dedicated pair of
eyes and ears for a company's hiring needs. A headhunter is
not bogged down with the administrative functions of HR
or other hiring departments. At its core, a search firm is a
sales organization. They sell information. They sell contacts.
They broker relationships. The result is putting the right
candidate in front of the right employer.

Due to this focus, a headhunter can be single-minded—
like a laser—finding those candidate attributes that fit a
company's expressed need. Recruiters may also run
employment ads in various media, but are better able to
respond *quickly* when they see what they are looking for.
Basically, it comes down to **eating**: an HR professional is
going to get a paycheck every two weeks regardless, whereas

a headhunter eats (gets paid) only when they place someone. There have even been occasions when, after getting the go-ahead from the candidate, I presented someone who had already submitted a resume to the *same* company and wound up making the placement simply because the company was *unaware that they had it!* However, another important function that a recruiter serves, which has had some companies pay me a fee even when they knew they had already seen a candidate's resume, is called *seeing beyond the paper.*

A good recruiter does not simply send resumes to clients. Outside the industry, those who do are lovingly called *paper-pushers* or *flesh-peddlers*. At a minimum, if a candidate fits one or more of a headhunter's current search assignments, he will spend some time with that candidate either in person or on the phone. Not only does he need to know much more than what is generally spelled out in the resume—reasons for leaving jobs, salary history, salary expectations, positions and industries desired, etc.—but the recruiter also needs to get a feel for the person's verbal presentation and personality. Some resumes simply don't look right for a position whereas, when connecting personally with a candidate and gathering more information, sometimes a possible fit can be seen. It's what I call "seeing beyond the paper." Though headhunters can't afford to see *past* the paper—resumes must bear *some* relevance to their openings—they may explore deeper when there's a glimmer of hope. This is part of the "value-added" service they provide to hiring companies. HR and other departments rarely manage to contact even highly desirable candidates from the resumes received, much less have time to see beyond the paper on others. With so little time, hiring managers often make split decisions based only on what they see in black and white. But resumes are impersonal billboards—they have no heart and soul.

People really want to connect with people, not paper

Although there is pressure on corporate departments to cut costs by cutting recruitment fees, there is a basic need of HR and other hiring managers to connect with *people*. Since they can't speak personally to every candidate, they are prone to connect with a trusted headhunter who can *tell* them about a great person. By getting the *heart and soul* of a candidate vicariously through interaction with a recruiter, a hiring manager connects with a person in a way that can't happen through a resume alone. Therefore, having someone "present" you to a company can be incredibly valuable, and the personality and quality of the recruiter through whom your information flows is a critical factor of success. In Part II, we'll talk more about this very important aspect of choosing the right recruiter: finding one that has earned the trust of major corporate organizations and is simply *liked* by clients.

The logistics of the recruitment process are rather straightforward:

- client describes a specific hiring need to recruiter
- they work out a fee arrangement for recruiter's services (contingency, retainer, or a middle-ground called "container")
- recruiter conducts a candidate search to fill that need
- after interviewing potential players, recruiter presents appropriate candidates to client
- client interviews candidates for possible employment
- if client hires a candidate presented by recruiter, a fee is paid

The fee is usually based on a percentage of the candidate's first-year compensation, though it doesn't come out of that compensation. For example, a 30% contingency fee means a company pays the recruiter a fee equal to 30% of a hired candidate's first-year earnings. A candidate hired at a salary of $60,000 with a $10,000 guaranteed bonus will net a recruiter $21,000 ($70,000 x 30%). Occasionally, the fee is computed solely on the "base" salary, or may even be a "flat fee" (e.g., $7,500 per Sales Rep hired). Compensation is the benchmark for determining the fee. Generally, placing higher-level, higher-priced professionals requires more work and expertise on the part of the headhunter and, therefore, commands a higher fee. There are other arrangements such as container and full-retainer agreements whereby a recruiter is paid some or all of the fee up-front, *prior* to beginning a search. In Part II, I'll discuss the contingency vs. retainer aspect of recruitment organizations as another consideration in choosing the right recruiter.

Finally, there is usually a "guarantee period" built into the company/recruiter agreement. This ensures that if, for some reason, the candidate does not work out within a certain time frame, the recruiter is obligated to either

> "I'd rather be a failure at something I enjoy than be a success at something I hate."
> —GEORGE BURNS

replace the person or refund all or a portion of the fee. Obviously, the headhunter is interested in the candidate making it through the guarantee period but, more importantly, in knowing that they have serviced both parties well so they are called upon for future hires. Today's placed candidate becomes tomorrow's hiring manager. Therefore, a good recruiter is less focused on the guarantee period than on long-term client and candidate satisfaction.

CHAPTER 2

Why Be a Hunted Head?

Headhunters get paid big fees for finding exactly what the client desires in an employee. Why, you may ask, should I use a recruiter? Could I perhaps get a higher salary by simply skipping that process, going straight to the company, thereby saving them a fee? In a word, no. Recruitment fees are built into company hiring budgets, and an avoided fee does not benefit a candidate. If they save a fee, it goes to the company—not to pay you more. (As you'll see, it may even be to your *detriment* if a company gets you for free.) Plus, salary ranges are usually pegged along a scale determined by qualifications, experience, and pre-existing company salary levels. Therefore, a candidate will not see any more money from a company-saved fee. However, there are many benefits in having a fee actually *paid* for you, some of which you won't realize until getting involved in a recruiter's placement process. Here I'll simply list some of the more tangible, immediate advantages of being placed by a recruiter:

1. Your resume, if faxed, mailed, e-mailed, or carrier-pidgeoned to a company, often becomes a millimetric addition to a mountainous stack of paper on some

hiring manager's or secretary's desk. Yeah—this is a *great* way to get noticed! Even though the business of headhunting requires staying on top of the flow of resumes so as not to "snooze and lose" a perfect candidate, recruiters can't help but accumulate piles themselves. Think of how much worse it is in an office with so much more to do than review resumes. I'll say it again: HR and other departments are too busy doing whatever else they do to get around to submitted resumes promptly, even if they ran an ad.

2. Another presentation benefit in being represented by a recruiter to a hiring company: you get *heard about* rather than only *seen* in impersonal black and white. There's a lot to be said for the sensory dynamics of hearing about someone and picturing them in your mind rather than sorting through descriptive words. There is room for personality, humor, casual friendliness—LIFE—to color the feeling that a hiring manager gets about a candidate in a verbal presentation that simply cannot be conveyed in the cold, hard world of ink and 20lb. bond. The "life" that the hiring manager feels is, for the most part, that of the headhunter. However, if the headhunter is a trusted, respected advisor to this company, that *surrogate* life can attach nuances of *feeling* to the candidate in the employer's mind.

Feeling . . .
nothing more than Feeling . . .

Obviously, it is important here to emphasize feeling. In many years of recruiting, I have grown keenly aware that, fitting within a certain range of qualifications for a particular position, *hiring decisions often come down to 90% chemistry and feelings.* So, the earlier in the hiring process that certain attractive feelings can be attached to a candidate, the greater the chance of an interview, if not eventual hire. A good recruiter attaches those feelings when presenting you to a company.

3. There is a financial-security benefit to being placed by a headhunter. Rest assured that a company willing and able to pay big money to a recruiter to hire you is a financially viable organization. You will find that companies with the savvy to utilize search services usually offer more attractive compensation and overall "packages."

4. There is an insurance benefit to being placed. Think about it: if they pay big bucks to hire you, how committed do you think they are to your working out? Having made an investment in you, they now have a tangible commitment to your success—more than to a person who wandered in off the street. Their effort to ensure your success is definitely colored by their not wanting to waste money. Sure, there's usually a window of time, a guarantee period, in which they could cut a candidate loose without incurring too great a loss. However, with all the legalities and other matters involved in the hiring/firing process, a company would seldom use this loophole as a "try them out" process—it just ain't worth it. When they hire you, they *want* you to make it. They're banking on your success.

Benefits of Being Placed:

GET NOTICED
PRESENTATION
FINANCIAL SECURITY
INSURANCE FOR SUCCESS

In addition to the benefits of being placed, you should be aware of the other services a headhunter provides:

1. **Hidden Job Leads:** Recruiters can put you in touch with immediate openings as well as opportunities arising later, when you might be looking more passively. This extra pair of eyes and ears alerts you to positions you might not otherwise access. Companies using recruiters often won't advertise directly, which is why headhunters deal in what has been called the "hidden job market." Though you shouldn't bank everything on a headhunter finding your perfect job immediately, it is nonetheless a potential source of leads to add to your own search efforts. A highly placeable candidate may be presented with so many opportunities that they needn't pick up a paper or move a mouse . . . a major consideration when trying to hold down one job while looking for another.

2. **Interview Preparation:** You will generally present yourself better to a potential employer after being coached by a headhunter on the company—what they are looking for and how to best address those needs in the interview. If you haven't looked for a job in a while, a simple brush-up to get into the "interview mode" is a lifesaver when putting yourself on the auction block again. Being reminded of the rules of the interview game and how it is played can quickly bring you back up to speed. Advice on attire, resumes, sample questions, opening and closing the interview . . . and much more are provided by the headhunter who, like an expectant mother, is anxious for you to deliver this baby.

   A recruiter's experienced insight into the mind and culture of an organization goes beyond company history and products/services, which you can research yourself on the Internet. While corporate research is valuable, a headhunter is often privy to the employer's *human* element—especially the people you might interview with. At the end of the day, this factor is often the clincher in getting a person hired.

3. **Negotiation:** How comfortable are you conducting face-to-face negotiations for a higher salary or more perks? Many may think they're pros, yet I would say all but the shrewdest salesperson would be hard-pressed to press hard, while remaining cool and composed, to successfully bump up the figures. First, you may feel that you actually *need* or *want* this job and, regardless of the words you use, *need* or *want* is easily perceived by a hiring company—to their advantage. Secondly, though you might be a great negotiator in your professional work, this particular negotiation involves *you* and *your* well being. It's darn-near impossible not to take that *personally* even when you know it's "just business." Here a headhunter assumes the impersonal role of intermediary to represent your best interests. Because their fee is generally based on your starting salary, recruiters have a vested interest in making the best possible deal for you. The more you make . . . the more they make!

I once placed a marketing professional with a software "giant" at a 33% raise over her previous salary, not including $20K in stock options thrown into the package. Though in the very business of marketing, she was nonetheless stunned when I conveyed the offer to her, having been fully prepared to accept a raise half as large.

---

4. **Buffering:** During the interview stage, and once you're on board with a company, a headhunter assists in the

new job transition by being a buffer of communication between you and the employer. Because both of you may have some initial perceptions or concerns that are not always fully expressed, the recruiter can relay and translate that information in a safe, professional way— alleviating potential problems before they arise. Recruiters often "save" placements by operating as a channel of communication between employees and employers. They have a vested interest because client and candidate satisfaction depends on a successful placement . . . as does their fee!

A Recruiter Provides:

HIDDEN JOB LEADS
INTERVIEW PREPARATION
NEGOTIATION
BUFFERING

CHAPTER 3

Staying Cool

When you're ready to make a career move, the urge is usually to do it as quickly as possible, right? Nothing wrong with a quick, calculated job change. But let me make a case, provided you weren't just laid off, for remaining fully and gainfully employed until you find your next position.

AS THE HEAD TURNS

Hedda's Office: Scene 2/Take 1

A C T I O N !

HEDDA HUNTER:	"Professional Search. May I help you?"
CANDY DATE:	"Hi! I'm calling to see if you can help me find a job. Who's the recruiter that handles Geothermal Oscilloscope Operational Service Engineers?"
HEDDA HUNTER:	"Uh . . . excuse me. Can you repeat that?"
CANDY DATE:	"Geothermal Oscilloscope Operational Service Engineers. I'm a G.O.O.S.E. Don't you place G.O.O.S.E.s?"
HEDDA HUNTER:	"[laugh] I think the plural is 'geese' but, I'm sorry, we don't."
CANDY DATE:	"Darn. You are the 63rd headhunting firm I've called and I can't find anyone to help me."

HEDDA HUNTER:	"Well, you are doing the right thing. I'd just keep calling different firms and asking them up-front if they handle that specialty. Your area of Engineering is just not our field."
CANDY DATE:	"Yeah, that's what I keep hearing from everybody. The bad news is, I already left my last job so I could focus on getting a better one. Things were just heating up so much around there and I got tired of the constant changes. So, I thought I'd be better off applying myself full-time to a job search. Now I feel so silly. Do you have any good ideas?"
HEDDA HUNTER:	"Have you thought of flying south for the winter?"

— **C U T !** —

Why risk being a cooked goose like Candy? After all, the recruiter specializes in looking at opportunities *for* you, very much like a Real Estate Agent when you search for a new home. Therefore, it's not necessary to use your own precious time when you could continue to earn a living in your own area of expertise. Now, if you are currently unemployed, much of the following will not apply—and try to not get depressed while reading it. However, if you are employed, stay with it! Before buying into some myth that you are better off pursuing a job "full-time," consider that:

1. A hiring organization always values something another employer has more than something it can get free. Call it human nature or whatever, but if something free is offered at your door, don't you wonder why? Companies do. I can't tell you how many times I've been asked "But why isn't he working?" Fortunately, in today's *candidate-driven* market (meaning

many more jobs available than quality people to fill them), this particular problem is generally not a death knell. Because companies are in such dire need of talent, they are more accepting of a candidate's reason for leaving their last job. Ironically, in less robust economic times, employers are even more emphatic about not considering those who are unemployed. They assume that there must be something wrong with the candidate (rather than with the economy). Also, in those *employer-driven* markets (many more quality candidates available than jobs for them to fill), as seen back in the recession of the early '90s, there are simply so many other good candidates available who *are* employed that it becomes a screening mechanism. It's a Catch-22, but in a recession, if you don't *have* a job, it's tougher to *get* a job.

> "The trouble with unemployment is that the minute you wake up in the morning, you're on the job."
> —LENA HORNE

2. Staying with your current job, you continue to earn a paycheck until you find the right opportunity. Hopefully your life is not simply about a paycheck. But it is a basic requirement that your financial needs be met while you are searching for that next perfect expression of who you want to be. Believe me . . . your decision will always be better when you come from a place of finding something that really *speaks* to you rather than settling for a job out of desperation.

3. By remaining employed, you're not sitting at home bored, anxiety ridden, going through the classifieds, or waiting for your headhunter to call with the perfect opportunity. Remember that sick, overwhelmed feeling in your gut the last time you scoured the want ads or

Internet when you needed a job *right now*? You knew the "process" meant that you were a long way from working—first sending out resumes, making follow-up calls, going on interviews, etc. Besides depressing, the classifieds are so damn cold and impersonal. Staying in your current job, you keep your mind occupied and less stressed about the transition. Less stress means better decisions.

Don't accept the notion that you can "focus" better on getting a new position by leaving your current one. If you are a strong, viable, marketable candidate, recruiters and employers will always flex around your schedule for interviews. Why? Because they always place greater value on a working candidate. If, on the other hand, you are not a "strong, viable, marketable candidate," then simply having more time won't help. Perhaps you will be able to bob around to interview with more headhunters, but there is little worse in salability than a less-marketable, out-of-work candidate. The "why unemployed?" question becomes a louder death knell. So, for both the strong and the not-so-strong candidate, the benefits of remaining employed far outweigh the perceived costs of time and frustration.

Don't bob—
keep your job!

CHAPTER 4

Am I Strong?
Am I Marketable?
Do People Like Me?

Well, the third question sounds like a personal issue, so I won't deal with it (at least not in *this* book). But, the question of one's market strength is worth exploring: can I, as a recruiter, sell you? It's fairly simple to answer—just ask. Of course, you want to ask the right person, as outlined in Part II, Choosing a Recruiter. You don't want to subject yourself to old-school headhunters who try to talk you down so they can gain "control" over you and your interests: they are easy enough to spot. You want to find straight-talking, *human* recruiters. Authenticity is also easy to spot. Just ask yourself "How do I *feel* when we interact?"

Then . . . after finding a straight-talker you trust:

1. make them feel *really* safe, telling them you want a no-nonsense answer—and can take it: many recruiters may write you off while playing nice-nice unless you ask outright for the straight dope

2. bolster yourself to hear their open, honest opinion without arguing or making your case (this will just shut down any openness you have fostered)
3. ask

The degree of comfort you deliver is the degree to which they will tell you exactly how you measure up in the market. And don't take just one person's opinion—as a matter of fact, you don't have to take *anyone's* opinion—but, if you really want to get an idea, this exercise will work. My advice, however, remains the same: stay put at your job, whether you're hot or not.

CHAPTER 5

Staying Sane

All that said, the question arises: "Darn it, Darrell—how do I keep myself from going crazy in a job I don't like while waiting around forever for a recruiter to find me a new one?"

Again, if you're a highly marketable candidate, it will not take too long to find another position, especially in a candidate-driven market. If you are not highly marketable, even if it takes a bit longer, your chances of being appetizing to a potential new employer are enhanced when you're currently employed. However, to preserve your sanity, I've advised candidates in each state of marketability to try this little mind trick: be a *temp* in your current position.

Have you ever noticed that when you are doing something to pay the bills that may or may not really interest you, like temping, there is very little stress involved? Basically, you just leave your job at the office at the end of the day and put your mind on other things. In the same way, though I am in no way advocating becoming a slug or giving less than your best in your duties and responsibilities, this little mind trick can go a long way toward preserving your sanity while doing something you are *mentally* done with. So, my advice is to "temp" along in your current position, viewing it merely as a transitional period until the right thing shows up. You may find the job itself isn't as bad as you thought. It may be the importance your mind is placing on being "in the right place right now" that is your real enemy.

This brings up the concept of *mind management* when it comes to finding another position. Temping at a current job is an example of how we must manage our minds during a job change. Similar to divorce, we have all seen people "lose it" when it appears that a basic foundational life structure is rug-pulled from beneath them. Many people handle career transition with this same destabilized attitude.

Some people wait until they "just can't take it anymore" to begin searching for a new position. A rather deadly approach, because desperate and frustrated job-seekers rarely do their best thinking. In Part III, Using a Recruiter, I outline the benefits of *always* having your updated information on file with your favorite recruiters (current resume, wish list of situations you're interested in hearing about, etc.). One very real benefit is for just this reason: you can hear about opportunities that fit your picture of the "perfect job" while being sane, productive, and somewhat content in your present position. First, you'll certainly make a better decision when you are relatively satisfied. Second, you don't have to re-invent the wheel every time you reach your limit at a job—your connections to other positions, namely your favorite headhunters, remain ever-active on your behalf. Both recruiters and employers find a happy, contented candidate much

> "Keep . . . your networking working, and your eyes and ears open for clues of changes coming that could be hazardous to the health of your career. Never stop looking out for number one."
>
> —HARVEY MACKAY, *SHARKPROOF*

more desirable than someone desperate to change. In addition, a candidate will often be wooed with more money, perks, etc., when being enticed away from an established, likeable situation.

A final point regarding mind management . . . adopt a *long-term* perspective when initiating a job change. By staying physically employed, and relatively mentally engaged (versus being checked out), you place yourself in a better position to find that new job which really calls to you. Waiting until the last minute to begin a search merely adds to the frustration of not "being in the right place." Don't jump from the frying pan into the fire. I repeat . . . the ideal situation is to *always* be looking. However, if you have just gotten to the point of no return in your present position, don't fret. First, remain calm—remember the "temp" mindset. That sets the tone for clear thinking. Then actively take the necessary steps starting up the search ladder. Contact your favorite recruiter, or interview new recruiters (with the interview techniques described in Part II). Give yourself a few months, at the very least, to consider new opportunities. Though your perfect position may actually show up sooner, you will be more calm, cool, and poised to land it when each and every interview is not make-or-break. You'll be able to be yourself and assess your choices comfortably. Adopt a long-term perspective.

> "Take calculated risks. That is quite different from being rash."
> —GEORGE PATTON

PART I
Candidate Basic Training Check-list

CHAPTER 1: Why Recruiter's Exist and What They Do

✔ Provide an outsourced pair of eyes and ears for client companies
✔ Operate with laser focus to identify quality candidates that fit their client's specific needs
✔ Present candidates beyond the paper to clients, adding life to a typical black and white resume
✔ Compensated based on—not from—the candidate's salary, so driven to the get highest $$ possible

CHAPTER 2: Why Be a Hunted Head?

✔ Because of the many benefits:
  ❏ Get noticed: You are distinguished from the crowd of job seekers
  ❏ Presentation: You get heard about rather than your resume only seen by a hiring company
  ❏ Financial Security: A company paying $$ for you is financially strong
  ❏ Insurance: A company paying $$ for you is committed to your success
  ❏ Hidden Job Leads: Positions handled by recruiters may be ones you wouldn't find elsewhere
  ❏ Interview Prep: Recruiters provide interview coaching along with an inside scoop on companies
  ❏ Negotiation: Recruiters are strictly-business advocates for your interests, getting you more
  ❏ Buffering: New job transition is supported through a recruiter's role as an information channel

CHAPTER 3: Staying Cool

✔ If you have a choice, keep your job until you find another because:
  ❏ Companies are more attracted to working candidates
  ❏ You keep your home together by earning a paycheck
  ❏ You keep your head together by having your mind engaged

CHAPTER 4: Am I Strong? Am I Marketable? Do People Like Me?

✔ Ask a straight-talking recruiter the first two—ask others the third

CHAPTER 5: Staying Sane

✔ Manage your mind during career transition by "temping"
✔ Think long-term: always update your resume with recruiters and give a job change time

PART II

CHOOSING A RECRUITER

*Finding the Right Place
to Lay Your Head*

Now that we have assessed the value of utilizing a recruiter as an avenue of career transition, it is important for you to learn how to choose one correctly. Yes, you can ask your friends which headhunters they know but, as in any profession, there are reasons why you would go to one service provider rather than another. The factors to consider range from specialty expertise and professionalism to personality fit, technological know-how, and state-of-the-art equipment. In the same way you would weigh all of these elements when selecting a physician, accountant, or attorney, you must take them into account in choosing a headhunter. A haphazard choice may indeed be hazardous.

AS THE HEAD TURNS

Hedda's Office: Scene 3/Take 1

A C T I O N !

HEDDA HUNTER:	"Professional Search. May I help you?"
LOU K. LOU:	"I'm thinkin' you might. I'm thinkin' you can. 'Cause if you've got a job, Louis is your man."
HEDDA HUNTER:	"uh . . . Excuse me?"

Lou K. Lou:	"Needin' to work. Willin' to toil—with the brass in the boardroom or the irons in the soil. Wantin' a job. Wantin' it now. Lou can do anything, if only shown how."
Hedda Hunter:	" . . . uh . . . [laugh] . . . do you *only* speak in rhyme?"
Lou K. Lou:	"I speak as I live: with a flow and a verse. I'm a free spirit flying, through the better and the worse. I know I've got talent. I know I can win. I'll do good for us all—as soon as I come in."
Hedda Hunter:	"uh . . . Well . . . uh, Mr. Louis, is it? Um . . . You see, we are a *professional* search firm. We don't deal in just *any* odd jobs—though *odd* might be the operative word here [clear throat]— . . . but, you see, we place professional-level individuals with specific experience into specific positions requiring that experience."
Lou K. Lou:	"I know what you're sayin'. I know what you mean. But you don't know what I'm made of until I've been seen. I'm better in person—up close, in the flesh—and as soon as you've met me, we're just gonna mesh. 'Cause you see, I'm a shaker, a mover, here and there, and once we've connected . . . "
Hedda Hunter:	"It'll be a nightmare. Thank you, and have a good day."

— C U T ! —

So, what's the point? Well, consider that, as a recruiter *or* candidate, you don't want to stay on the phone with just anybody—much less meet them. There are just some types that you won't "mesh" with. Getting caught up in the wrong crowd can be a major waste of time . . . and potentially dangerous. Just as in all relationships, there are certain signs to observe when evaluating a possible match. The right tools will give you the ability to judge where to best invest your time and effort in headhunter relationships. So, here are some tools, methods, and insights delivered straight from an insider to help you affiliate—and "partner"—with the most appropriate recruiters. In effect, you'll learn how to "interview the interviewer" to discover whether a prospective recruiter is right for you.

Before bringing out the toolbox, however, let me introduce the idea of "partnering" with a recruiter. I discuss this in much greater detail in Part III, but consider for now that headhunters can be much more valuable in the long run if utilized with an eye *toward* the long run. Too often, professionals operate from the shortsighted mentality of either 1) I'm looking for a new position *right now,* or 2) I'm not looking at all. If actually looking in this "emergency" mode, the choice—or non-choice, as the case may be—of which recruiters to use is rushed and lacks planning. It becomes: "I'll work with whomever calls me with something that sounds interesting; I'll work with whomever answers the phone when I call the search firm; I'll work with whomever is willing to talk to me if I'm out of work; I'll work with whomever." Rarely, if ever, would you put your long-term best interests into the hands of a "whomever" doctor or attorney. Why, then, do so many professionals put their long-term career interests into the hands of "whomever" recruiters?

Two reasons. First, because most professionals operate in the above-mentioned black-and-white world, they are often caught off-guard when it comes to needing a headhunter. For reasons of loyalty to their current employer, they consider themselves absolutely unavailable until the day they want another job *immediately.* So, they are left semi-desperate, if not dazed, when beginning to look for a recruiter. Even if not desperate, these professionals don't engage their best business mind in assessing the qualifications of a head-hunter in the same way they would assess any other vital service provider. Hence, the second reason professionals resort to this indiscriminate mode of allowing just anyone to handle their career is simply because they don't know how to choose a recruiter *responsibly*. Choosing responsibly is what this section is all about.

In all matters of choice, it's the choice that matters

CHAPTER 6

They Pay Me Now or They Pay Me Later

Recruiter's have an infinite number of specialties—those industries or professions they serve. However, there are essentially only two types of search organizations, the distinguishing factor being the payment plan: Contingency (payment at the end of a successful search) and Retained (payment up-front—either partial or in full). And believe me, how *they* are paid impacts directly how *you* are paid (whether you get a job through them *so as to get paid*). Each form of recruitment organization operates under a different context or set of eyes and ears. Consequently, your approach to them must be different. The following breakdown will shed light on the vital differences between contingency- and retained-search firms.

Contingency

- Paid for services only after successfully placing you; in effect, your recruiter works for *free* until the time their client firm hires you

- Usually offer some "guarantee" period to clients, which means that their fee payment only becomes free and clear once you *prove* yourself by staying with a company for a certain time period—akin to a manufacturer's warranty
- Deal with a variety of assignments (positions to fill) at the same time
- Includes organizations from the "employment agency" level, placing more clerical and support staff, all the way to executive search firms placing only upper management
- Conduct searches for positions with base salary levels of $18,000 to $100,000 or more
- Focus on serving the client company, yet more likely to press them on your behalf: because they only get paid when someone is hired, they may work a bit harder to get a marginally appropriate candidate seen by the client, on the off chance that there could be a fit

Retained

- Paid for services up-front, either partially or in full
- May not offer guarantees to their clients, so once a position is filled, they are off the hook
- Concentrate on fewer assignments with a more limited client base
- Operate as a "consultant" to their clients—hired to render advice, not just resumes
- Place specifically high-level executives at salary levels usually above $100,000
- An "exact-fit" candidate is already paid for by the client, therefore they are less likely to press on your behalf: though retained recruiters would like to complete their assignments as soon as possible, they won't present marginal candidates

Now, at first blush, it may appear that retained search is the way for recruiters to go: apparently more security in payment, less guarantee liability, and more of the client's ear. However, first impressions don't always reveal the full picture. For many practical business reasons, there are viable numbers of both types of search firms in today's world. Many contingency-search firms are exactly that because of the freedom it affords them to work with whomever they want/when they want, without being tied to specific assignments or agreements. *The Directory of Executive Recruiters, 2000 Edition* by Kennedy Information, Inc.—commonly referred to in the search arena as the "Red Book"—listed 3,337 firms categorizing themselves as contingency and 1,667 as retainer. Though this listing is in no way exhaustive, it gives a sense of the broader issues pertaining to the benefits of each style of organization. Over the past 20 years, more contingency firms have been presenting themselves to clients as retainer organizations. They are just as capable of conducting retained searches, but of course don't have the reputation of such retained-search icons as Korn-Ferry, Heidrick & Struggles, or Russell Reynolds.

The point is not to debate the merits of recruiters operating in either contingency- or retained-search structures. For you, the candidate, it is simply important to know that this distinction can impact your success with a particular firm. Here is the deciding factor in knowing which type of firm will best serve your needs:

Your Professional Level
(not your level of professionalism)

Don't worry much about working with retained-search firms if you're below a 6-figure salary level. These firms are not organizations you would necessarily "go sign up with"— they deal with whomever *they* choose. If you are a 6-figure professional, you might submit your resume to a retained firm for inclusion in their database. However, the general rule for dealing with them is: don't call them—they'll call you. They are paid up-front to go out and find specific talent. Rarely has anyone in their "files" fit a particular assignment. If they need you, *they'll find you.*

On the other hand, contingency recruiters focus on professional positions with base salary levels ranging from $18,000 to well over $100,000. Even if they engage in some of the same assignments as retained-search firms, their operations are generally more open and less exclusive. It is far easier and possibly more fruitful to get into a contingency firm's database. They work on a greater number of assignments, necessitating greater dependence on their files. Since contingency recruiters are only paid when the placement is made, they don't enjoy the retained firm's luxury . . . lot's of time to focus on fewer assignments. They must quickly locate as many people as possible with the potential of filling any opening—before being beaten to the punch by some other contingency recruiter. Therefore, they search their database and consult their files regularly. And because of the drive to get paid, contingency headhunters are more apt to stretch for you, hopefully to get you on interviews for positions for which you may have been overlooked by retained-search firms. This is not to say contingency firms do sloppy work—it just means that, because they enjoy no payment until after the placement, they may be more prone to find possibilities or angles to present a candidate who doesn't fit the client's standard profile.

All of this simply says: for the average professional—and of course there are more professionals in the $18-100K range than in the over-$100K range—a contingency-search recruiter is going to provide a greater probability of success. Don't let this general rule throw you off, however: if a firm claiming to do retained search wants your resume, send it.

Send it to *anyone* expressing interest, provided they meet the selection criteria in the following chapters. Know, however, that you're simply not going to be contacted or placed by a bona-fide retainer firm unless you lie in the precise crosshairs of their sight. A contingency recruiter's "scope" may view a slightly broader target.

CHAPTER 7

Listener vs. Round-Hole Filler

A critical element in determining the right headhunters for you is noticing the ratio of **words** coming **out** of their mouths compared to **words** going **in** their ears. You might call it the **WO/WI** factor. (Easy to remember because, "Wowee! Man, does that guy talk a lot!") In addition to the *ratio* of words being exchanged, there is an issue of the *timing* of that exchange. To illustrate:

AS THE HEAD TURNS

Accounting Department: Scene 4/Take 1

A C T I O N !

UNA WEIR:	"Accounting. This is Una."
ANITA FIIH:	"Hi Una. My name is Anita. Look here, Una, I'm a recruiter with WTYL Search [We Talk You Listen]. We're one of the foremost professional recruitment organizations on this side of 4th Street—east of Lincoln Blvd., that is. I wanted to introduce myself and see if you have a moment to speak."

UNA WEIR:	"Well, uh . . . it's not really the best time to talk . . . my hands are . . . "
ANITA FIIH:	"Kinda full, huh? I understand, Una. You don't have to say another word. I understand the lingo. I've been doing this kind of call for years. You don't want the boss to hear, right? Well look, how about I just tell you why I'm calling and you won't have to say a thing—just listen. Una, I'm working with a really big client in your industry that is looking for an Accountant to do just what you do and is willing to pay a lot more than you make. Are you interested?"
UNA WEIR:	"Well, . . . I guess I'm always interested in moving more in that direction."
ANITA FIIH:	"Great! So, tell me Una: what does your company do, what exactly do you do there, and what do you make money-wise?"
UNA WEIR:	"I don't know *what* they do, but *I'm* the receptionist, and [whispering] *they pay me dirt!* How much can I get with your client? Will they teach me accounting, or do they really just want me to "do what I do" here? It doesn't matter— it'll be cool to even just have the title: Accountant! But, I really have been wanting to learn. That's why I started temping in this department yesterday. I guess this is just my lucky day, huh? And to think, I wasn't going to pick up that call because my nails were still drying. Life's funny, isn't it? . . . Hello? . . . Hello?"

— C U T ! —

What's wrong with this scene? Well, first of all, this call seems a little indiscriminate, don't you think? Sweet little Una just happened to be the lucky (or unlucky) one to pick up the phone. Not necessarily a bad thing, if the recruiter were interested in getting to know *Una* and what *she* is up to/interested in. However, Anita was only intent on filling the particular job that she had on her desk at the moment. Again, not necessarily a bad thing, because this is always a headhunter's main motivation. But a headhunter's interaction with a potential candidate reveals volumes about how they work. A WO/WI factor greater than one (more words going out than in), at least in the beginning, can be a sign of greater disregard to come.

Anita is a Round-Hole Filler, so intent on filling her current opening that she doesn't even try to involve herself with the interests, desires, and needs of her potential "candidate." She would like to fit *anyone* into her round hole, no matter how square a candidate might be, simply to make the placement and get her fee. Anita is probably someone to avoid unless, of course, the particular position she's hawking at that moment interests you. One thing you can count on: if that position doesn't interest you, you will probably hear about many more that don't interest you. Anita is not someone you would call a "career partner." She is more of an "any job quickie."

> "The reason we have two ears and only one mouth is that we may listen more and talk less."
> —Anonymous

A key factor in partnering with a recruiter is whether or not they take the time to listen to your needs and desires. Many candidates get frustrated dealing with recruiters constantly calling them about positions that don't fit their stated desires. The best way to deal with them? Don't deal with them! The headhunter for you is the one who gets to know you, your interests, and your needs during the first phone-call and then only contacts you with opportunities that fit those criteria. Therefore, the WO/WI factor, in the beginning at least, should be small—ideally a ratio of less than one. Although recruiters may initially focus on and espouse the merits of a particular opportunity, you need to get a quick sense of whether or not *your* interests are being probed—or are they just trying to fill a hole. Whether you're a match for that particular position or not, good recruiters always want to build their database with potential future candidates. Therefore, they want to know what would really turn you on.

WO/WI of 3 = Commercial! Catch zzzzs!
WO/WI of 2 = What's missing is you
WO/WI of 1 = Extremely more fun
WO/WI of less = They pass the first test

When you connect with a good recruiter who gets into your interests and desires and, over time, tells you about positions that fit those interests and desires, stick with 'em. But don't expect that headhunter to have immediate opportunities that fit—unless you want your corners rounded to fit a hole. Finding the perfect position may take some time, especially if you're quite specific about what you want. Keep in mind that greater flexibility on your part leads to your recruiter calling you with more possibilities. A good rule of thumb: two calls from a recruiter to whom you've spilled your super-specific guts with positions that don't fit, move on to someone who listens. However, if you bare your soul to a recruiter who doesn't call back for a while, if ever, either 1) they listened well and can't help you, or 2) they are simply still looking for a position that fits. In either case, there is less wasted time on your part. Wouldn't you want your recruiter to spend time trying to *find* opportunities for you rather than easing your insecurities? It won't make anything happen faster to be on the phone *telling* you that they don't have anything for you. If you haven't been called, assume there is nothing yet to call you about.

Although a recruiter is paid by her client companies, a good search professional operates with two customers in mind: the company *and* the candidate. You might call the company the "client" and the candidate the "customer." Just know that a good recruiter understands that to really forward things in this life—the client's, the candidate's, the recruiter's—it's best that everyone be pleased with a placement. Candidates who have had their edges shaved to fit particular round holes eventually become dissatisfied, even if they work out relatively well in the short run. This means they have to move to other jobs, and the company must find other people to fill their positions. Although there is a misperception that this is the *ideal* scenario on the part of the headhunter (the "churn" factor), someone who operates on this Ride-'em-in/Ride-'em-out philosophy will not succeed for long. A recruiter's reputation among clients and candidates is determined by each party's satisfaction with a placement. Real success is built upon this kind of reputation. You want to "partner" with such a recruiter.

CHAPTER 8

Trust and Clout: Trout!

When you start fishing the waters for recruiters, focus on a good "trout" stream because Trust and Clout are two determinants of a winning catch. Let's first consider trust.

Do you sense that you can trust a particular recruiter? Is he trusted by his client companies? The more you can answer these questions regarding a potential "career partner," the better. On a personal level, the gut speaks volumes that the mind can't always absorb, so you may just need to go with it. Client trust, however, may be more difficult to determine given that many headhunters will not necessarily divulge their client's identity until absolutely necessary. But here is the very nature of the beast: if they are reticent to reveal the names of clients they service, it may reveal something about the strength of foothold established with those clients—an indicator of the level of trust and clout in those relationships.

> "The best way to tell if a man is honest is to ask him. If he says he is, you know he's a crook."
> —GROUCHO MARX

Don't blame a recruiter for not spilling all their proprietary-information (client list) when first meeting you. After it has been determined that the two of you might be a good working match, this should not be an issue. Some head-hunters, as in any service industry, might even have letters on file from former satisfied clients or candidates. It's not a must, but it might be an avenue to explore in determining a recruiter's muster.

Another simple way to assess the trust factor—turn an oft-used interview question back on the recruiter: "What would your candidates say about you as a recruiter? What would your clients say?" Initially, it might throw the head-hunter off to be interviewed by a candidate. But, whatever the outcome, you win: either 1) the recruiter is caught off-guard and reveals a power-trip men-tality which says "I am in charge, not you;" 2) they reveal an interesting perspective of themselves that you can process through your own BS detector; or 3) your chutzpah and professional savvy in asking makes an incredible impression, upping their desire to work with you. As I said, whatever the outcome . . . you win.

> "It is unfortunate, considering that enthusiasm moves the world, that so few enthusiasts can be trusted to speak the truth."
> —A. J. BALFOUR

A word about trust: it's a two-way street. Don't expect a headhunter to let her hair down and begin revealing more than the usual cryptic information unless and until you are willing to do the same. The successful recruiter/candi-date relationship is founded on the same principles as all human relationships—mutual trust, mutual respect. If you view a new recruiter through past-tainted glasses, know that what you see will be tainted. Best to always be the one to demonstrate trust by sticking your neck out first. This opens the gate for reciprocity. What are some recognizable elements of trust? Basic openness, honesty, and authenticity—letting your guard down to let someone really get to know you . . . where you've been, where you want to go.

When considering the trust dimension, it is important for you to know a recruiter's basic fear when disclosing client information. It's that the candidate will go around the recruiter, doing an end-run straight to the company. I'm sure those reading this book have more integrity than that. But to understand the motivations and mindset of a headhunter, know this: "going around" means that the candidate takes the information gained from an initial conversation with a recruiter and uses it to contact the hiring company, thereby bypassing the company's obligation to pay the recruiter's fee. As low-down as it seems, it does happen, and the fear has been genetically ingrained in headhunters, whether or not they've actually experienced it. You see, recruiters are in the *information-brokerage* business: they broker the information they gather on clients and candidates to make a living. If a client or candidate utilizes information gained from a recruiter to either hire an employee or get a job, unquestionably that recruiter is entitled to compensation.

> "And trust me not at all
> or all in all."
> —ALFRED, LORD TENNYSON

If, on an initial call, you've ever asked a headhunter "What's the name of the company?" and you've heard him hem and haw, now you know why. Certainly you have never entertained the thought of using such information unethically but, on the first call, a recruiter doesn't know you from Adam. Over time, as in any budding relationship, when the candidate and recruiter learn more about one another, more is revealed. So don't be offended if you can't find out everything up-front—understand the headhunter's situation. In time, however, if an open and relaxed relationship between recruiter and candidate has not begun to coalesce, there may be reason to reassess your choice of recruiters.

Now let's take a look at clout.

THE PRICE UPON THEIR HEADS

The question arises in venturing out:
What bounty to place on a headhunter's clout?
To choose a pro player, not loser or lout,
The highest, the Highest, the HIGHEST no doubt.

Webster's New Collegiate Dictionary defines clout as "pull" or "influence" and it is another vital ingredient in your total recruiter evaluation picture. One way to determine it is by asking outright "What is the range of fees you charge client companies?" Again, it may well elicit surprise, a candidate turning the interview tables, but the reaction will be revealing. A headhunter who is highly respected by clients is well paid. She may not want to reveal this information, claiming that it is proprietary in nature. Don't let this be an immediate turn-off: your relationship may not yet be at that level of openness. Then again, it may mean that this firm is a "bargain shop," a cut-rate recruiting house that undermines the professionalism of the entire industry by charging fees far below average. If you were proud of your services, don't you think you should enjoy the privilege of charging prevailing rates?

It is questionable whether recruiters charging fees less than 20% in a candidate-driven market (except for volume business) are at the top of their profession, or so regarded by their clients. A headhunter accepting low fees, when there are zillions of companies needing recruitment services, has little regard for the importance of what they do. This equates with the headhunter version of the ambulance-chasing lawyer. Most professional recruiters, respected by their clients, charge proper industry fees (25-35%). They offer experience, ability, service, and professionalism. Again, this percentage rule does not apply as strongly to certain "volume" placement work, when a recruiter makes multiple placements with the same client, or in an employer-driven market, when there are fewer jobs to fill, dropping the average fees charged by recruiters.

You may well say, "What do I care what fees the head-hunter charges, so long as I get the interview and land the job?" Well, I'm not saying it carries all the weight of your determination, but consider this: would you rather go to work for a company strong and financially capable enough to hire the Neiman Marcus-style recruiter, or for a company so frugal as to shop only at Wal-Mart? What is the "price vs. value" mentality you would like your future employer to have? Nothing wrong with saving money, but will this reticence to pay for top professional service reveal itself later in the company's relationship with *you* as a valued employee?

Another determinant of clout focuses on whether or not this headhunter has the influence and connections to place you in positions commensurate with your qualifications and experience. Again, this is easily assessed by turning the interview tables on the recruiter and asking "Can you please tell me the professional and salary levels of your last 4 placements?" Be prepared for the headhunter's "Excuse me? Who do you think you are?" response, in voice or facial expression. If you have earned your stripes by being one of the best in your field, you can easily get away with this. A recruiter truly dealing with individuals at your level should be willing and able to give you relevant examples. If, however, they squirm and have nothing to offer, you might be dealing with someone in a league of their own—not yours.

A final divining rod leading you to clout is a recruiter's professional designations, affiliations, and associations. In any profession, distinction is often made by a smattering of letters after individuals' names. **PhD**, **MBA**, **JD**, **CPA**, **CFP**, and **MD** degrees and certifications signify particular expertise and training. So, too, do the letters **CPC** and **CSAM** help identify professionals in the recruiting world. A **Certified Personnel Consultant (CPC)** has passed a series of rigorous exams covering ethics, professional recruitment knowledge, and employment law. This exam is administered by the National Association of Personnel Services (NAPS), the oldest trade association of the staffing industry. Much like a CPA, a CPC must be maintained through continuing education credits, earned by attending professional training seminars, completing educational coursework, etc. A **Certified Senior Account Manager (CSAM)** is a designation specifically used within the firm of Management Recruiters International (MRI) to recognize top consultants who, again, have passed certain educational and effectiveness requirements. However, keep in mind: letters don't buy you everything, and lack thereof is not necessarily a black mark. It is just one of many available criteria to use in evaluating a professional in any field.

After noticing if the recruiter you are considering has "lettered," you might also inquire about affiliations and association memberships. In addition to participating in trade associations such as NAPS, there are many professional and cooperative "networks" to which a headhunter might belong. They serve a continuing educational purpose and encourage a team approach to the business, resulting in split placements (one recruiter providing the candidate, the other the client). Not only do all members profit more by working together than individually, they also broaden their service capabilities. For example, three associations to which I belong—National Personnel Associates (NPA),

First Interview, and Recruiter's Online Network (RON)—connect me with thousands of recruiters nationwide, and worldwide (See Appendix C). This way, I can provide a wider service, drawing upon the pooled "products" of my networked affiliates to find what would fit my client's and candidate's needs in *any field*, in *any place*, at *any time*. Some of these associations are very exclusive, requiring certain standards of professionalism, successful track record, history of teamwork, and ethics to gain admission. Notwithstanding the statement of professionalism such membership implies for a headhunter, it also serves to connect you with more resources from which to draw in finding your "perfect job." Therefore, a recruiter who works and plays well with professional colleagues will net you better results—and greater long-term career management.

CHAPTER 9

Systems Savvy Search

Another consideration when determining your headhunter "partner" is their utilization of the latest technology. When it comes to the recruitment process in the 21st century, your chance of success with a recruiter will hinge on their ability to manage the flow of information in an intensely information-overloaded world. Now, you can walk down the street to Jack & Myrna's Job-On-A-Stick to get that "personal touch," where all candidate information is written by hand on cardstock, each desk has a Rolodex with well worn, frayed cards of client companies, and the concept of RAM is what they try to do with a job down your throat. There will be, however, certain sacrifices you will make regarding the caliber of companies you'll be presented to based on your recruiter's "worldly" knowledge. Your choice.

My recommendation is to assess your recruitment firm's credibility and viability in the rapidly changing job market by their ability to perform in the hi-tech, corporate world. This means, simply, **COMPUTERS** and all the accoutrements: e-mail, Internet, scanners, keyword searchable databases, etc. Initially, this may seem to identify a more impersonal firm. Not true. The degree to which a search firm utilizes these technologies impacts their capability as a player in the recruitment field and reveals contemporary understanding of the world in which we live.

AS THE HEAD TURNS

Hedda's Office: Scene 5/Take 1

A C T I O N !

HEDDA HUNTER:	"Professional Search. May I help you?"
LOIS TIEM:	"Yes, if you don't mind. *Of course she doesn't mind!* I'm not sure, but I believe I'm listed in the system as person number 8360793 and I wanted to check in on something. My name is Lois."
HEDDA HUNTER:	"Lois, [chuckle] you may be in our database, but we don't track our candidates by number. What was it you wanted to check on?"
LOIS TIEM:	"You see, I wanted to inquire about a job I saw listed on the Internet under your firm's name. If it's OK, . . . *Will you stop groveling for crying out loud!* . . . um, I'd like to hear more about position number 1313MBL that you had posted on the Munster Board. It was listed in the Maryland section."
HEDDA HUNTER:	"uh . . . You know, Lois, we don't keep track of positions by number either. Those are just randomly assigned by the listing Web site. Uh . . . Can you tell me what the position was?"
LOIS TIEM:	"I'm really sorry but . . . *Quit with the apologies already!* . . . I don't remember the title. It had something to do with 'case studies' and 'in-depth analysis.' Those are both things I'm familiar with."
HEDDA HUNTER:	"uh . . . Oh! You mean the Market Programs Analyst position in the D.C. area. Lois . . . is . . .

	uh . . . that a field you have . . . experience in?"
Lois Tiem:	"Oh, yes, if I do say so . . . *Just say so! Just say so!* . . . um, I've been involved in countless programs, one of which focused specifically on me getting out more by spending time at the market—to be more comfortable with people and crowds, you know . . . *She knows! She knows! It's written all over your face!*"
HEDDA HUNTER:	" . . . uh . . . "

— C U T ! —

You must admit: it takes a lot to leave Hedda Hunter speechless. Just remember, utilization of high technology in the workplace does not necessarily mean impersonal service. A technologically efficient office signifies just that: efficiency. A firm that manages information well wastes a minimum of your time locating your "perfect job." Service, whether personal or impersonal is, frankly, a *personal* issue—unique unto each headhunter. It has nothing to do with the systems employed. Yet, your adaptability to the recruiter's systems aids tremendously in obtaining the best service.

The "instruments" utilized in your potential "career doctor's" office should involve computers. The days of managing information on index cards or in manila folders are gone. There is only so much information-capacity/memory that any human can handle. Yet, a recruiter's ability to quickly retain and locate information is a crucial determinant of success. It's true that Jack & Myrna, who've placed people with the same 6 clients for 20 years, have no problem tracking their client/candidate information manually. Yet, as I said earlier, at Job-On-A-Stick, your exposure is limited to their 6 companies.

Computers, and the myriad accessories that accompany them, allow for information management, retention, retrieval, and transfer. Technology enables a headhunter to stay efficient, effective, and sane in this hurly-burly world. Whether it's a recruiter's ability to receive your e-mailed resume (which gets your information into "play" faster) or their ability to research company information on the Internet, *all things technological* create more success in landing a job through that recruiter. Would you want a headhunter probing his memory or poring through office file cabinets to recall you when your "perfect job" arises; or, would you rather he had the ability to access your information systematically and with greater alacrity through a keyword searchable database? Of course, it's crucial that you set yourself up to be *found*, or retrieved, from that database by structuring your information in a certain way. However, through the use of technology, your chance of hearing about the ideal position is much higher than if you depend upon human hardware (memory) alone.

> "Technology has replaced hot cars as the new symbol of robust manhood. Men know that unless they get a digital line to the Internet no woman is going to look at them twice."
>
> —SCOTT ADAMS,
> CREATOR OF *DILBERT*

Basic "hunting gear" to notice when initiating talks with a headhunter:

1. **Computers! Computers! Computers!** Just be sure they aren't some old dinosaurs with black and green Cathode Ray Tube (CRT) screens. Outdated systems mean outdated technological capabilities.

2. **Keyword Searchable Database.** There are many different types of information-management software

packages available for recruiters. Those requiring "coding" and data-entry of your information are less efficient than systems based on *keyword search* and result in your lowered exposure rate. Contemporary systems can input your entire resume into the database, allowing it to be retrieved anytime a keyword search is done calling for your experience, credentials, or interests. (Part IV covers resume construction that helps you take advantage of these technologies.)

3. **E-mail/Internet Capability.** It's simply the communication medium for today. A headhunter *not* utilizing this resource is like a stockbroker using the telegraph instead of the phone—or the phone instead of on-line trading!

4. **Scanners.** These flat, small, copier-look-alike devices "scan" your resume into a database. While not the most efficient form of data transferal, it at least attests to a firm's knowledge and utilization of contemporary technology. Scanners were more critical before e-mailing resumes became popular (an e-mailed resume plops neatly and immediately into a database), so it may not be utilized as regularly now. But whether it's collecting dust or shoved into a corner, the fact that the firm *owns* a scanner shows that they have been awake.

You may find some or all of these items in any particular office. Just keep in mind that there are advantages to working with technologically adept search firms. Knowing what tools to look for and ask about can point you in the right direction. Then, trust your gut as to whether or not a recruiter has systems savvy.

CHAPTER 10

Being That Special Someone

This last point may seem simplistic; nonetheless, it warrants discussion. Many job-seeking professionals waste valuable time and energy contacting or mass-mailing/e-mailing recruiters who have no interest in them based on "specialty." You wouldn't go to a shoe repairman to get your teeth cleaned. So, as a software development engineer, don't send your resume to a recruiter specializing in sales and marketing professionals. Of course, in today's cheap-communication world where a batch of 50 e-mails can be blasted off at the click of a mouse, a candidate may not consider it a terrible waste of time. But, when you consider all the e-mail addressing, personalizing, and cover letters to prospective recruiters—and it's apparent when it's *not* personalized (a.k.a. "spam")—it adds up. (Please note that "spammed" resumes, whether sent by yourself or some service that indiscriminately blasts them out for you, are not highly regarded. Can you say 'junkmail?' I thought you could.)

Don't waste your time dealing with headhunters who can't help you. It's too frustrating—especially if you're really ready to move. Just make a minimal effort to determine a firm's specialties before initiating or expanding on a relationship.

I'm always amazed to find recruiters specializing in virtually every professional, or non-professional, area of employment. From editors to educators, nannies to nuclear physicists, warehouse workers to Windows NT programmers, I have seen every kind of specialty being worked in the field of headhunting. Knowing this, let wisdom prevail— assess each particular recruiter for the ability to handle placements in your field.

This assessment is not brain surgery, however. Make it easy on yourself with a simple, initial call to a search firm asking about their special area of expertise. You might also refer to *The Directory of Executive Recruiters, 2000 Edition* (the "Red Book") which you'll find in any bookstore or library, or check online at http://www.kennedyinfo.com (See Appendix C). In addition, when you deal with systems-savvy recruiters, there's a high probability that they have Web sites that outline their focus areas. If a headhunter contacts you out of the blue, ask him up-front. These simple measures will help you concentrate your efforts in directions that promise the highest return.

CHAPTER 6: **They Pay Me Now or They Pay Me Later**

✔ Two types of search firms, Contingency and Retained, operating with different eyes and ears

✔ Retained firms focus on $100K+ professionals and contact *you* if interested—don't call them

✔ Contingency firms focus on $18-100K+ professionals and utilize candidate submissions

CHAPTER 7: **Listener vs. Round-Hole Filler**

✔ The Words In/Words Out (WO/WI) Factor is critical for having your needs and desires met

CHAPTER 8: **Trust and Clout: Trout!**

✔ Letters of reference from former satisfied candidates or clients?

✔ Interview the interviewer:
  ❏ "What would your candidates say about you as a recruiter? What would your clients say?"
  ❏ "What is the range of fees you charge client companies?"
  ❏ "Would you please tell me the professional and salary levels of your last 4 placements?"

✔ Professional designations/affiliations can signal a greater ability to serve you

✔ What does your gut tell you about working with this recruiter?

CHAPTER 9: **Systems Savvy Search**

✔ Computerized, database-driven firms may provide more possibilities for successful placement

✔ Items to look for:
  ❏ Computers, computers, computers
  ❏ Keyword searchable database
  ❏ E-mail/Internet capability
  ❏ Scanners

CHAPTER 10: **Being That Special Someone**

✔ There are recruiters out there specializing in whatever you do—find *them*, work with *them*

PART III

USING A RECRUITER

Putting Your Head to Work

You now have a sense of why to use and how to evaluate a headhunter. As you survey the field of players, you may ask yourself, "How do I capitalize on this process?" The answers that follow relate to your "ownership" of the *tool* of using search firms to assist in your job change.

As with anything you bring into your life, you want the benefits of that item and, therefore, must be responsible for its use. Take, for example, a dog. You want to enjoy the love, playfulness, and vitality that dogs bring to life. So, you get one. Then, of course, being *responsible* for your dog means that you clean it, feed it, and keep it healthy. Similarly, there is a way to utilize recruiters responsibly which yields you, the candidate (or customer, if you will), the greatest benefits.

> "No man is born into the world, whose work is not born with him; there is always work, And tools to work withal, for those who will."
> —JAMES RUSSELL LOWELL

A rather unique definition of "responsible" may shed light on this idea. Consider being responsible as *being the cause of something.* In marriage, for example, most successful relationships are approached as a 100%/100% proposition, rather than 50/50. So too, you will personally benefit from fully *causing* the success of your recruiter relationships. Congratulations! You've started by reading this book. When you've completed it, rather than being at the mercy of those anonymous people, you can have your own sense of control in dealing with them. This section gives you the ideas and mindset to be *in charge* of successful relations with headhunters.

> "If you want good service, serve yourself."
> —SPANISH PROVERB

> "The best way to predict the future is to create it."
> —PETER DRUCKER

CHAPTER 11

Own Your Own Business

No, this section is not in the wrong book. Do you think, because you are "employed" by a company that hands out paychecks, the concept of owning your own business does not apply to you? Think again. Think hard. Think beyond what you've thought before.

"BUSINESS." What does it mean? Well, let's simply break it down: busy-ness—the act of being busy. Do you stay busy? Do you engage in activities all day long in your workplace which keep you busy? O.K., then there is your busyness. We each have our own busy-ness. The question is, how much do you *own* your own business?

Ownership is an interesting concept. It puts you in charge. Rather than being dependent upon something or someone greater than you, ownership puts full responsibility for what you produce squarely in your lap. Along with that responsibility, however, comes the opportunity for great reward. Consider all the entrepreneurs out there creating their own companies. It's the old tradeoff of risk and return: the more we take responsibility for our own success and assume the onus of producing results, the greater, more satisfying the potential rewards.

We all won't become another Bill Gates or Warren Buffet, and "owning your own business" does not even mean starting a company. (If everyone started a firm, there would be nobody to work for anyone else—then *I'd* be out of a job!). You bought a book about using headhunters wisely because you work for someone else, right? Nothing wrong with working for someone else. But I am asking you to consider that you already *have* your own company: [**YOUR NAME**], **Inc.** After all, Webster's New Collegiate Dictionary defines "incorporated" as "united in one body." I am asking you to adopt the mindset that you are *self-employed*. I am suggesting that, to the degree that you, as an employee, *own your own busy-ness*, you will reap greater rewards, because staying busy doing *anything* for *anyone* without always fully knowing your value and options is *not* good business.

AS THE HEAD TURNS

Hedda's Office: Scene 6/Take 1

A C T I O N !

HEDDA HUNTER: "Professional Search. May I help you?"

ERNEST ZACHARY PICKENS: "Well I sure hope so little lady. You see, I'm new to this here town and I'm lookin' for a place to rest my bootable floppies. [chortle] . . . Just a little humor there, sweetheart . . . "

HEDDA HUNTER: "[groan] . . . what a day . . . "

ERNEST ZACHARY PICKENS: "Excuse me missy?—I missed that."

HEDDA HUNTER: "uh . . . oh, I said "Well, . . . good day!"

ERNEST ZACHARY PICKENS: "You can bet your last Indian-head nickel on that. It *is* a good day! I ain't felt this fired-up since old man Jacobs lit up the seat of my pants with buckshot after keeping Weida Mae out all night."

HEDDA HUNTER: "uh . . . yeah . . . . .um, Mr . . . ?"

ERNEST ZACHARY PICKENS: "Ernest Zachary Pickens, ma'am, at your service. Please call me E.Z. though. That's what my friends do."

HEDDA HUNTER: "[under breath] *Oh, you do have friends, huh?* [clear throat] Well, Mr. *E.Z.*, just what can I do for you?"

ERNEST ZACHARY PICKENS: "Well, little darlin', like I said, I'd like to get to work and start earnin' my keep. I had the idea that you might be able to help me? What do you think—what's say we paint this here town green?"

HEDDA HUNTER: "[nonplused] . . . um, . . . yes, . . . what a lovely thought. What exactly do you *do*, Mr. *E.Z.*?"

ERNEST ZACHARY PICKENS: "That's *exactly* right. What is *exactly* what I do. You say *what*, and I'll *do* it—faster than a cold bath 'for church on a winter weekend."

HEDDA HUNTER: "uh-huh . . . . . . So, ... you don't care, right? It could be *anything*, right? *All someone has to do is* **tell** *you what to do and you'll* **do** *it, right?!*"

ERNEST ZACHARY PICKENS: "Sweet thing, you just name it, and it's done. It's over. It's history. It's so done it's plum burnt."

HEDDA HUNTER: "O.K., . . . then pay attention. Listen closely now. *Get that ear real close to that phone!* **GET A LIFE! JUST GET—A—LIFE!** [slams phone down] I mean, *what's* going on today? I'm getting Ricky Rhymes, then there's Sybil, and now Jethro! What ever happened to simple, everyday candidates? If this keeps up, *I'm* going to be looking for a job myself!"

— **C U T !** —

73

Don't be easy pickings—own your own business. What do I mean by that? Just this: you have certain assets, right? As a professional employee, much less as a human being? Those assets could be your award-winning sales ability, your keen and persuasive public-relations skills, your ability to multi-task the elements of a busy desk, your fluency with programming code in the most difficult of computer languages, your knack for hiring the right person for the right job, your unique and motivating management style, your sense of numbers which has all the pieces of the financial puzzle come together, your engineering acumen in the face of the most challenging circumstances . . . . I could go on, and I've only touched on *professional* abilities here—not to mention innate, personal strengths which single you out as a unique, special person.

So let's accept that you have certain "assets." Well, what does a business do with its assets? It deploys them in such a way as to maximize their profitability, right? The success of an enterprise depends most on its ability to utilize its assets, to "employ" them, to invest them wisely to reap the highest return. In the world of finance, it's called Return on Investment (ROI). The higher the ROI for a particular group of assets, the more successful the business—enhancing the *owner's equity* and causing happier owners, stockholders, etc.

You, a *self-employed* business owner, invest your assets in the employment "market." Whether you invest them here or there makes all the difference in the ROI you will receive. You might consider your own business's ROI as Return on Effort (ROE) or Return on Ability (ROA). Your owner's equity, or "career equity," will be impacted by your choice among investment opportunities. The degree to which you *own your own business* and, therefore, focus on managing your assets most effectively, is the degree to which you will get the most career satisfaction—and profit. So, the question becomes:

Where are you going to put *your ass(ets)?*

When used responsibly, recruiters can be viewed as brokers —investment advisors showing you the myriad career investment opportunities available. You put your paycheck, your money, in the bank so it can be managed by someone else, enabling you to deal with other things, right? Maybe you send it to your stockbroker so she can put it in the market to net you the highest return. Whatever you do with it, you place it in someone else's hands so you can focus on what *you do best.* There is nothing different about using a good headhunter to help you invest your *employable assets.*

Now, I'm not suggesting that you, as an investing employee, should shift your "portfolio" every time the employment market moves a particular way. In the world of Wall Street, as in life, work, relationships, etc., holding a steady course and riding out the bumps is often the best option. However, if and when the "writing on the wall" gets too big to be ignored, is it not better to have someone who has continually watched the market for you assist in moving your assets elsewhere?

> "What is the first duty—and continuing responsibility—of the business manager? To strive for the best possible economic results from the resources currently employed or available."
> —PETER DRUCKER

This ability to prudently re-invest, however, does not come from the old-style use of recruiters—on an emergency basis. You wouldn't expect a doctor to know everything about how your body works the first time you walk into his office, nor would you want a stockbroker you just met to arbitrarily throw your money into this or that fund, would you? No. You would want a doctor to be fully informed about your medical history and have some personal, long-term experience observing your health. You would expect a stockbroker to know your long-term financial goals when determining your best investment portfolio. Similarly, to use a recruiter responsibly and have your long-range welfare taken into account, you want to establish a long-term relationship with that recruiter. I'm not suggesting that emergencies won't occur when you will need a recruiter's help right away. However, to the extent that you've been a regular "patient" or "investor," you will often get better service.

CHAPTER 12

Career Management/ Partnering

Why do major sports figures, Hollywood celebrities, writers and artists have agents and "personal managers" handle their careers? Because they want to focus on doing what they do well. They don't want to bother with watching the market for the next best opportunity to play their particular game, express their particular craft, or capitalize on their particular talent. They want to *know* about that next best opportunity . . . they just don't want to spend time looking for it.

Why regard your abilities with any less value than they regard theirs? Sure, they may make more money, but it's the principle that counts. Maybe they *make* more money because they have given responsibility for strategically deploying their strengths to someone else. Your talents are just as valuable, in their own way, in their own "optimal employment."

The key to careers being fully enjoyed
Is keeping yourself optimally employed
Ensuring this happens requires someone who
Discovers great jobs—while you do what you do

> "Money isn't everything
> as long as you have enough."
> —MALCOLM FORBES

A word here about optimal employment. Greater compensation is one potential benefit from reinvesting your employable assets wisely, but know that money is not the only consideration in a career change. Celebrities also utilize career management professionals to locate opportunities showcasing their unique talents that may not always involve more money. Similarly, you may direct your employment portfolio in ways that net you a higher return in whatever "returns" you want most. This could mean making more money, but it could also mean a shorter commute to the office. Your best return could come in the form of a more challenging work environment, or even an entirely new line of work. Interesting studies over the last decade have shown that "quality of life" is the highest priority in making a job choice, not money. So, whatever floats your boat in terms of desired return from assets, you can seek out that particular return for your optimal employment.

> "Anyone who
> thinks money will
> make you happy . . .
> hasn't got money . . .
> Happy is harder
> than money."
> —DAVID GEFFEN

The point is: how do you best seek it? Sitting on your ass(ets) at one particular job until the day they wake up

> "Never take a job in a place where you can't
> throw cigarette butts on the floor."
> —ANONYMOUS

your ass(ets) by letting you go doesn't get it done. Listening to other opportunities for your talents only when you are, if not physically, *mentally* unemployed because there's simply no juice in your current job—also a poor method. Effectively pursuing the most goodies for your gifts means taking a *proactive* posture, as would any businessperson running a business, any "star" running a career.

I always tell candidates "You are never going to take a job unless it's right for you, but it never hurts to look." And it never hurts to hear. Yet there are responsibilities that come along with remaining thus open. You'll have to sacrifice the blissful ignorance of being uninformed of sweeter deals elsewhere. You'll have to make *decisions* about your career. (*AAARRRGGGHHH, I have to decide something!*) At times, you'll have to endure the discomfort of telling those around you that you are leaving to play in a better sandbox. But, the benefits of being so responsible far outweigh these standard, if unattractive, duties of running a business.

> "We are CEOs of our own companies: Me Inc. To be in business today, our most important job is to be head marketer for the brand called You."
> —TOM PETERS

This is a wake-up call, meant to jostle you before you experience a ruder awakening. Until you take entrepreneurial command of your own value, your career will never give you all it could. Let's be clear: overly opportunistic job-hopping is not the approach being advocated. Recruiters, like companies, are not attracted to rubber resumes, which show more bouncing than Tigger on my son's Winnie the Pooh videos. No—constant movement for the sake of only a little more here or there is not smart. Sometimes in the long run, enduring the rough spots and staying satisfied is the best way to go. But calculated movement, based on a long-range career plan, coupled with ongoing opportunity awareness —*this* is a winning strategy.

Pay attention to what's out there: you never know when it might be you!

Be informed about relevant options as they arise, based on your overall career objectives. You might be at the job you just started for 10 years, but if another position surfaces that *totally* fits your wish-list, your "dream job," you should at least know about it!

Yet, even if you agree that it never hurts to stay open to having your wish-list granted, a thousand recruiters out there calling you takes you away from your job and what you do best. So just pick a few. In the same way your favorite sports figure or actor has trusted, well-informed agents and managers directing the way to their next gig, long-term recruiters can guide you. Definitely have a few because one headhunter can't ethically place you into and recruit you out of the same company—but he can sure help you the next time around! Career Management or, as I like to say, Career Partnership, isn't a privilege for only the rich and famous. It can be a privilege for *you*. And, best of all, it costs you nothing!

> "Life is too short to live with a bad deal."
>
> —DAVID GEFFEN

"What? How does that work? I get someone seeking to have my highest career dreams realized at no cost?"

That's right. Remember: the fee paid to recruiters *is not* deducted from your paycheck. It is simply *based* on your pay. Your deal is even better than that of the "stars," who dole out 10-15% of their take to agents and managers.

What a deal! What a bargain! Lucky you!

Though my firm performs nationwide placement, on a local basis there are several professionals I've had the privilege to place 2 or 3 times—always after their call informing me of their need to move again, for one reason or another. The best part of placing them has been becoming "family:" spending time together socially, attending each other's significant life events, having our children participate in extra-curricular activities together, etc.

In order to "partner" with a headhunter for your long-term best interest, there are actions you must take to create and maintain that relationship. From romantic relationships to delicate pieces of machinery, regular maintenance keeps things running smoothly. Whether it's taking your significant other on a date once a week or changing the oil in your car, these procedures help *ensure* that everything keeps working to your satisfaction. Similarly, following certain guidelines will enable your chosen career partners to best support your lifetime career goals. Read on!

"Take a chance on romance. Even if you're secure in your job and not seeking to make a switch, you may change your mind if the right opportunity comes along. If a recruiter offers you a discreet interview with someone who has expressed an interest in you, consider exploring the jungle. You could be pleasantly surprised."
—HARVEY MACKAY, *SHARKPROOF*

CHAPTER 13

A Day in the Life . . .

A favorite lesson from the classics of cinema can be found in "To Kill a Mockingbird," the 1962 film starring Gregory Peck. At one point, Uncle Atticus tells his young daughter, Scout, that she will get along better in life by learning one simple trick: you only really understand people when you consider things from *their* point of view—when you get into their skin and walk around in it. Similarly, to best understand and appreciate the value of "relationship maintenance," it is helpful to have a feel for what goes on in a headhunter's typical day. So, let's explore the nature of the beast you are courting—or being courted by.

Recruiters organize their days in various ways, all centering around certain basic activities. A headhunter, you might say, manages the flow of several *pipelines*, which must stay full, alive and vibrant if the business is going to be successful. With any of these pipelines out of commission, the headhunter is out of commission—and, consequently, *earns* no commission. A recruiter focuses on balancing these activities and increasing the flow in each of the following pipelines:

1. **Searches:** Searches are the life-blood of a recruiting organization. Without specific positions to fill, the headhunter is out of business. Therefore, a major thrust for a recruiter is continually obtaining searches through all manner of marketing, cold calls to potential clients, existing client account servicing, referrals, and advertising.

2. **Candidates:** Of course without qualified and appropriate professionals to fill those openings, a headhunter is headless. So, recruiters constantly and vigorously pursue all avenues to add heads to their storehouse of possibly placeable professionals. Whether a candidate is *sourced* (obtained) indirectly through a Web site, newspaper ad, or referral, or directly through that always exciting cold-call to an unsuspecting professional, a successful headhunter is unceasingly managing a flow of contacts, relationships, and resumes of viable candidates.

3. **Send Outs:** It's great (and essential) to have an ongoing flow in the first two pipelines, but if they are not coming together as Send Outs, you're looking at one inefficient, ineffective recruiter. Send Outs are exactly that: sending out a viable candidate on a viable search. The initial hurdles of the placement process have now been cleared:

   a. A company has found a presented candidate interesting enough to interview

   b. A candidate has found a presented employment opportunity interesting enough to interview for

   c. A recruiter, who has done all the presenting, has established a specific time and place for the interview (The ultimate matchmaking, yes?)

4. **Placements:** This, *this* is what a headhunter's life is all about. We enjoy developing relationships, having fun, living our daily lives, but we are in the business of, and

stay in business only by, making placements. In a perfect world, placements are those magical moments when, as in dating, everything clicks so well with both parties that two pieces of the puzzle snap right into place. Unlike marriage, the candidate and company are not committed to spending their lives with one another, yet they are definitely going steady. Unfortunately, the placement process is not always so "magical" and requires the experienced mediation, management, communication, and even arm-chair-psychologist skills of a recruiter—not to mention sales ability. Making placements and closing deals is a headhunter's all-encompassing pipeline activity.

Note: it takes a greater volume in the first pipelines to result in any volume in the last. Because of the sieve effect of the first 3 pipelines (Searches, Candidates, Send Outs), there must be much more activity in them to net any Placement activity.

As illustrated in The Recruiters Pipeline on page 86, picture the pipelines with holes along their sides, where an incredible amount of "leakage" occurs throughout the system. Despite the leakage from the Search and Candidate pipelines (jobs getting filled; candidates taking other positions; no matches for either—85-90% or more of the volume!), some actually converge into Send Outs. Though the odds get better here, depending on the experience and effectiveness of a particular headhunter, there's still substantial drainage from the Send Out pipeline (employer or candidate not interested in the other). Recruiters often gauge their effectiveness by a statistic called the Send Out/Placement ratio. More effective recruiters will have a lower number of Send Outs to Placements (say, 3 to 1), while those less effective will have a greater spread (say, 10 to 1). Even with continuing Send Out leakage, albeit at a slower rate, some Send

The Recruiter's Pipeline

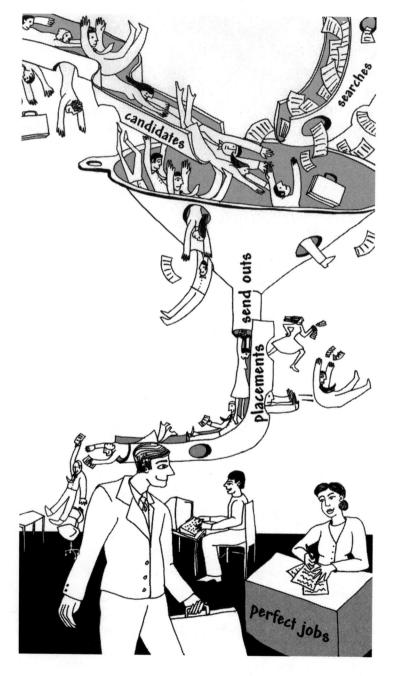

Outs actually become Placements. The "date" (or multiple "dates" in some cases) actually turns into a committed relationship.

Once the Placement is made and the employer/employee bond established, a certain amount of loss still occurs. For various reasons—perhaps one or both parties failing to reveal their true selves during the initial interview period, mind changing, finding a better prospect elsewhere, etc.—one or the other decides that this relationship just ain't right! To some extent, these situations reflect the relative effectiveness of the headhunter. If it occurs within the *guarantee period* that is usually part of the company/ recruiter agreement (e.g., 30 days), you then have a "Fall Off," which to a recruiter can mean anything from a need to replace that candidate free-of-charge to not being paid at all for work on that placement.

Yes, a hard, cruel reality in the headhunting business is Fall Offs. But, despite the pain and sense of wasted effort, recruiters keep doing what they do. Call us gluttons for punishment. Yet, the payoff on the deals gone sweet not sour— the ratio of which depends on the professionalism and effectiveness of the recruiter—makes it all worthwhile!

An added dimension to this process is the cumulative effect of recruiter "networking." Headhunters can't always rely on their own storehouse of heads/clients to provide either the right candidate for a particular search or the right search for a particular candidate, so they often work deals with each other. Just as real estate agents split commissions on home sales when representing buyers and sellers, headhunters split placement fees. For example, if I provide a candidate who another recruiter can place, or vice versa, we split the fee, 50/50. This type of networking occurs both on the *inside,* within small or large recruiting firms (where headhunters in the same company split deals), as well as on the *outside,* between independent and separate recruiting firms. Quite simply, a recruiter's pipeline management is not based solely on personal activity (obtaining searches; finding qualified candidates; arranging Send Outs), but is exponentially increased by the amount of networking in which the recruiter engages.

This may all sound foreboding and requiring an Act of God to have a placement occur. The truth is they occur all the time. Considering the management-, professional-, or salary-levels of searches a headhunter engages in, he can place anywhere from 2-6 individuals a month. Yet for 2-6 solid placements to materialize from that intricate network of leaking pipelines, there must be an enormous amount of "substance" continually going through the system. A successful recruiter's office, you would think, must be a literal hub of activity, a huge transfer facility, so as to direct enough substance into these pipelines. You are right! So, next time you call into a recruiting firm to chew some fat about yourself, remember that you just dialed Grand Central Station!

It is important for you, the candidate, to understand this movement within a recruiting organization to determine how to best position yourself to utilize this resource. Understanding the flow that a headhunter is attempting to manage on a daily basis allows you, to a certain degree, to step into her shoes and walk around a bit. Between the ongoing activities of a recruiter fishing for searches, sorting through resumes, hunting new heads, arranging interviews, and consulting/counseling both clients and candidates in this important decision-making process—most of which takes place on the phone—you want to slip in as smoothly as possible. The remainder of this book covers the "relationship maintenance" actions that will position you for greatest results when partnering with a headhunter.

CHAPTER 14

Recruiter Etiquette

Given all I've described about the hub of activity that characterizes a headhunter's office, it is important to know what "manners" will enhance your relationship with that headhunter. First and foremost, understand that recruiters are in business to make money. Given a choice, we would place *everyone*. So, know that our antennae are constantly up to sense and grab any opportunity to earn a fee. We would *love* for you to be our next placement. Perhaps you will be. Odds are you won't.

It's simply statistics. Again, when looking at the leakage that occurs in The Recruiter's Pipeline, you must figure, realistically, that the odds are against you. However, does that mean that it's not worth the try? Absolutely not! In the short run, if you need a job *today*, using a headhunter is, at the very least, another *possible* way of landing your next position, with all the benefits attached. However, in the long run, and more in line with the idea of

> Always be nice to people on the way up; because you'll meet the same people on the way down.
>
> —ANONYMOUS

career partnering/ career management, if you simply want a hired-gun pair of eyes and ears observing the vast, ever-changing market of career opportunities for you, a recruiter is a very solid investment.

The point is: I probably won't be able to place you immediately. Yet, if you needed a job yesterday and contacted me today, at least you've initiated a possible relationship. Who knows—I might have something! If not, with the myriad number of searches I will see over the long term, both from my own clients and those of my networks, I'm certainly going to come across *some* opportunities that will interest you. Over time, I may place you. The problem is that many professionals don't parlay this shortsighted, emergency need for a job into the more profitable, long-term payoff of an ongoing relationship with a headhunter. Thus, they eliminate the greatest benefit available to them from the recruiting industry: lifetime career management.

As headhunters, we want to help you, yet the odds are against our placing you immediately. So, how do you best interact with a recruiter to forward the long-term process? Here are some ideas to consider, reminiscent of what we learned in kindergarten:

1. DON'T BE PUSHY

    Don't try to *force* yourself onto a recruiter, and **don't cold call** to start the relationship—unless you just want submission information (fax number, e-mail address) or to inquire about specialties. Recruiters need a resume *first* to know if it's worth the time to talk. Submit yourself and several days later make a follow-up call, if you like, to confirm receipt. However, know and trust that you *are* being reviewed and considered to the best of a headhunter's ability. Hounding him won't make him work any more efficiently and will get irritating—not the best way to get started. After submitting, if you don't receive a response within a reasonable time frame (2-3 weeks), it probably means that he can't help you because either 1) he doesn't have any current openings for someone with your background, or 2) he deals in specialties different from yours. It does you no good to have him on the phone *telling* you that he doesn't have anything for you—that is time he could be using to *find* something. Believe me, if you have chosen your headhunters wisely, your resume will not go unnoticed. But time is precious, so recruiters can't hear every person's personal story until there exists a potential search that fits.

Remember: headhunters focus on finding candidates *for the searches they currently have,* which often require very specific qualifications. Your resume alone gives the recruiter enough information to make that determination. If you don't fit a current assignment, but may well fit a future one, she will keep your resume in the database or even give you a call. But she won't spend as much time with you then as she will when and if she actually has a search that might be a match for you. So be certain your resume and cover letter give the recruiter explicit details about your background

---

"Never, ever treat a recruiter rudely. They have very long memories. The recruiter you dump on today could be the person you're calling tomorrow or next week for help in finding a job. Do you think that person will be eager to return your call after you've banged the phone down on his ear? There's always another candidate. Burn your bridges and you're going to be looking for a life raft."

—HARVEY MACKAY, *SHARKPROOF*

and future interests to enable her to foresee the best possible match.

> People can be extremely emotional in a job search—especially when times are tough. Some handle stress better than others. Believe it or not, during the recession of the early '90s, when there were few hiring companies, a candidate grew so frustrated at my having no opportunities for him that he stopped calling twice a day and actually burst into the office demanding that I send him on an interview immediately. Unable to conjure one up out of my hat, the only placement I was forced to make was a restraining order on the poor guy.

2. MAKE FRIENDS

Try to establish a friendly connection with a recruiter any time he initiates contact with you. If he hasn't contacted you, refer to Item 1: Don't Be Pushy. Friendly relationships keep you in the forefront of a headhunter's mind. If you are a top candidate in his area of specialty, *he will always want to be your friend.* Even if you are only marginally valuable to him for placement purposes, an amiable connection on a personal level can help you in countless ways by reserving more of his consciousness for you. Recruiters talk to candidates all day. You want to do *anything* to instill more awareness and memory of you (short of proposals of marriage, reciting Shakespeare, etc.). I can't tell you how often I've spoken to candidates who've approached *me* (as opposed to my approaching them through a recruiting call) who interact with me as just another cow in the herd of headhunting cattle. If you're talking to *that* many recruiters, you're bound to grow cold and numb.

Limit the field of recruiters you court so you can always appear fresh, open, and receptive to their overtures. But, if you're going to blanket your resume throughout the recruiting world, at least be prepared to *smile when they dial*. To "partner" with a headhunter for the long term, you want to feel comfortable with one another as soon as possible.

3. ONE GOOD TURN DESERVES ANOTHER

Take any opportunity to provide a favor to a recruiter, not as an opening to be *used*, but as an opening to *schmooze*. If you have developed, or are developing, a potential ongoing relationship with a headhunter who calls for, say, some referrals for a particular position she is trying to fill (commonly known as "bird-dogging"), point the way for her if you can. You might even offer names of companies you hear are hiring, friends or coworkers who are planning a career move, etc. This kind of favor only serves to put *you* in greater conscious awareness with that recruiter. Don't think in negative terms, such as "she wants my help, but she can't place *me*." If she could help you, she certainly would. But, given that she can't, for the

---

"Be a resource. Now that you've got a
headhunter's name on your Rolodex,
make sure your name is on theirs.
Make it known that you'll be happy to assist
them in their searches, coming up with names of
possible candidates or companies. By helping
them for now, you've helped yourself for later."
—HARVEY MACKAY, *SHARKPROOF*

moment, establish a greater friendship by doing a good turn, which could serve you well. What goes around, comes around.

4. **DO UNTO OTHERS AS YOU'D HAVE THEM DO UNTO YOU With Trust:**

Trust is a basic factor in choosing a headhunter. Yet human relationships are always a two-way street. It's sometimes difficult to determine how far to go in trusting someone until you've formed a solid, trusting relationship. Which comes first, the chicken or the egg? Basically, it is incumbent upon one of you to take that first step. Remember, there is always the dilemma of the recruiter, cautious about spilling his brokerage beans too soon—his client information and contacts. A headhunter does have to gain a certain sense of safety before baring all. You, the candidate, can help establish an atmosphere of trust through your manner of interaction. Be open with your recruiter about everything. What you say will not always make it to the client (e.g., what you *really* thought about your last boss, etc.). Yet, it is important for a headhunter to be completely *in the know* when sticking his neck out for you with clients. Your level of openness can only foster greater personal rapport, which *always* comes back to serve you. Consider that any job opportunity lost by being open with your recruiter was not your opportunity in the first place. Headhunters are bright! Their intelligence is born, in part, by financial motivation— if they can *ever* see a way of placing you, *they will.* But, if they say a position is not right for you, based on your disclosed information, it only saves you wasted time and effort.

To engender a relationship built on trust, be prepared to:

- Describe, indepth, *all* of your background (not just what appears on the resume)
- Show a W2 for your last 2 years of employment and a paystub to verify salary
- Tell your recruiter about all pending interviews/offers so they don't cover the same ground
- Spend time prepping and debriefing around interviews
- Provide contact information for references (ideally former managers)
- Provide degree verification information
- Disclose any criminal, legal, or credit issues that could arise in a background check

The point is simple: don't waste your time or the recruiter's. Layout your cards as they are and trust that all will be done to play them right.

With Honesty:

Be honest, straightforward and tell your recruiter *everything*. Leave no skeleton closeted! You and the recruiter can decide together just what information is pertinent to your candidacy with a potential employer—and what can remain unsaid. A headhunter is an expert *packager*. You might describe some simple aspect of your personal or work history which the recruiter can package, or spin, in such a way as to render you more attractive to an employer—while at the same time maintaining complete honesty. Therefore, you want your headhunter armed with all the ammo needed for either the preemptive strikes or defensive maneuvers required to present you in the best possible light. Never let a recruiter be caught off guard, which happens when the client, in an interview, uncovers one of your dark secrets that you didn't share with the recruiter. In that case, the headhunter cannot help you because it shows she didn't really know her product . . . you! The very same information, artistically packaged by the recruiter in advance, could be conveyed preemptively and rendered less harmful.

With Courtesy and Respect:

Just keep your word. Do what you say you are going to do. Yes, if you deal with every Tom, Dick, and Harriet recruiter out there, perhaps it will be difficult to meet all your agreements. But if you have chosen selectively, simply honor your commitments and follow through with scheduled phone-calls and interviews. How you interact with headhunters is an indicator of how you conduct yourself professionally. Don't blow your image with your image-maker.

CHAPTER 15

Regular Check-ups

Goin' & Startin's Laff-In

PATIENT: "Hey Doc! I just started a job and can't sleep at night."

Doc: "How come?"

PATIENT: "Because I'm sleeping at my desk all day!"

Ba-dump-bump

PATIENT: "Hey Doc! I have a pain that keeps showing up at work."

Doc: "Where is it located?"

PATIENT: "In my boss's chair."

Ba-dump-bump

PATIENT: "Hey Doc! There's something going around my office."

Doc: "What is it?

PATIENT: "Advancement. Everyone's catching it but me."

Ba-dump-bump

PATIENT: "Hey Doc! Things are tough at work. I need a fiscal exam."

Doc: "You mean a physical exam."

PATIENT: "No. It's my checkbook. It's not breathing and I'm worried."

Ba-dump-bump

A healthy you requires regular visits to your dentist and physician. Use the same wholesome approach in your career. "Visits" in this arena, however, assume physical form not in actually going to see your "career doctor," but in always having your updated resume on file. Now, listen up!

I said always *on file . . . which means . . . ALWAYS!*

As soon as you begin that new job, during your very *first* week of employment, even if you don't yet know exactly what you're supposed to be doing, incorporate at least the job's "description" into your resume and get it over to your favorite recruiters.

"What?! Are you crazy, Darrell? Start a new job and immediately begin looking for another? That sounds like something a typical headhunter would say!"

No, I'm not crazy. I did not say begin looking for another job. And that is not what a typical headhunter would say. Rather, it is what a progressive, *career-partner* headhunter would say.

No matter what position you just landed, rarely, if ever, have you been left *wish-less* in life. Maybe the commute is better, but not ideal; or the position is close to what you want to be doing, but not exactly right; or the money is good, but you can't help feeling you're worth more; etc. I'm not preaching dissatisfaction or suggesting you go into your new position with anything less than full enthusiasm and motivation. I'm not saying that this opportunity isn't the *perfect* one for you *for the next 10 years!* I *am* saying that, even if you just started a new job, the time to update your resume and wish list and get them over to your career partners is *anytime* something in either of those documents changes.

Here's the rationale. First: if your absolute *dream job* showed up tomorrow, with exactly the location you desire, the responsibilities you want, or the greater compensation you've always felt you deserve —even if you just started a new job yesterday—it's important to hear about it! I'm not advocating less than total commitment to your current situation. *I'm simply suggesting that you always stay fully informed of other situations.* It costs you nothing to know the market! Smart investors stay abreast of the stock market each day, but that doesn't mean they constantly shift their portfolio.

> "If a window of opportunity appears, don't pull down the shade."
> —TOM PETERS

Similarly, rather than develop a "rubber" resume, bouncing from one place to the next, choose your employment investments wisely. Know that great opportunities don't stop showing up just because you've already taken a job. Remember: you're never, ever going to take another position unless it's right for you, unless it provides something more, better, or different that you really want. Just stay informed! Be *in tune* with the world around you and *in touch* with your headhunters so you aren't oblivious to any possible ideal situations that arise.

> "We pay for security with boredom, for adventure with bother."
> —ANONYMOUS

Even if you never change jobs again, at least you are either 1) continually validated in your choice of employment by constantly hearing how much better you have it, or 2) fully informed of what is out there to possibly parlay that information into more goodies from your present employer. Just as recruiters extract information from you when asking for referrals (bird-dogging), you too can use information gleaned from them to better your lot in your current job. You either make what you have better, or you leave for better. It's a no-lose proposition! This gives rise to the best definition I've ever heard for my profession:

Headhunter = Messenger of Opportunity

(what you do with the message is up to you!)

Of course, you don't want to spend your entire workday hearing about other jobs, especially if you're not actively looking. So, don't update your information with everyone. However, have a few chosen headhunters receive your most current information so that at least *somebody* is ensuring that your dream job doesn't slip by. Sincere, well-qualified career partners will only call you with opportunities you should *absolutely* know about.

There's another reason for getting your updated resume and wish list over to your headhunters immediately, even during the first week of a new job: if you don't do it now, you'll forget. Trust me, you *will* forget—and you'll lose the diskette!

> "I skate to where I think the puck will be."
> —WAYNE GRETZKY

Once you become so submerged in your new position that you can't see the light of day, you'll lose all consciousness of the big, wide world out there with so many opportunities. You'll totally forget the energy, dynamism, and living-on-the-edge nature of being in the job-search mode. Nothing wrong with being submerged, especially if you're happy. It provides that comfortable sense of security, stability, and predictability we all desire. However, the bad news is that you don't come up for air again until the water gets polluted—until you want, and *need*, to get out *now* (company layoff, corporate "restructuring," drowning in the job, etc.). This "emergency" career management is never the route to long-term growth and development. Sure, you might get lucky and fall into a great job. But it's far better to be poised to hear and consider all great opportunities fitting your wish list *whenever* they come up.

Learn to manage your career proactively, never reactively. Before you forget the fresh skills of resume preparation and design, put another one together. Also, taking into account the territory you've gained in accepting this new position, create an updated wish list—with an eye already focused on what's next in your career. Then, *and only then*, you can afford to submerge yourself in the duties and responsibilities of your new job. Once you know a lifeline is out there, with a trusted partner managing your breathing apparatus, you're assured of the vital connection to the world above the surface.

> "Procrastination is opportunity's natural assassin."
>
> —VICTOR KIAM, WHO LIKED REMINGTON SO MUCH HE BOUGHT THE COMPANY

In addition to updating your resume and wish list as soon as you start a new job, keep your recruiter continually abreast of any changes. Anything, *anything at all* that alters your status, should be shared with your recruiter in revised documents.

This process serves three purposes:

1. A headhunter is always incorporating your most recent information into her search criteria. A new address, employer, title, responsibility, certification, accomplishment, or interest appearing on your resume or wish list could well mean the difference between your hearing about a new position or not. Why? Because of

keyword searchable databases, which scan the entire text of a resume for specific words used in a headhunter's search.

2. You stay vigilant about managing your assets. Constant updates in the hands of your recruiter keep you aware of your current valuation and demand in the market. If a revised resume serves only to consciously document *for yourself* that you own your own business, like preparing a balance sheet of your assets, then it has served its purpose.

3. Being updated, you are physically equipped with the necessary tool (your resume) if and when a perfect opportunity arises. Having to create one in a pinch, when you've lost the diskette, is a manic process.

"You miss 100 percent
of the shots you
never take."
—WAYNE GRETZKY

CHAPTER 11:   **Own Your Own Business**

✔ Being responsible for your company's success, **[YOUR NAME], Inc.,** means investing your employable assets wisely

✔ Utilized long-term, a recruiter is an investment broker, ensuring the best return on your assets

CHAPTER 12:   **Career Management/Partnering**

✔ Your ongoing optimal employment is enhanced by partnering with a recruiter

✔ You won't always move, but it never hurts to hear about opportunities out there

✔ Establishing "career partner" relationships beats emergency career management

CHAPTER 13:   **A Day in the Life . . .**

✔ Recruiters manage several leaking pipelines: Searches, Candidates, Send Outs, and Placements

✔ This hub of activity must be considered when creating/maintaining recruiter relationships

CHAPTER 14:   **Recruiter Etiquette**

✔ Manners for partnering with a recruiter:
   ❑ Don't Be Pushy—being overly aggressive may be a turn off
   ❑ Make Friends—set yourself apart in the recruiter's mind
   ❑ One Good Turn Deserves Another—extend a favor, it can come back to you
   ❑ Do Unto Others As You'd Have Them Do Unto You—with trust, honesty, courtesy, and respect

CHAPTER 15:   **Regular Check-ups**

✔ **Always** update your recruiter when anything in your career or contact information changes

✔ Constant updates → more job-market info → wiser business ownership

✔ Manage your career proactively, not reactively

PART IV

HI-TECH
HEADHUNTING

*Resumes for
Database Jungle Fighting*

When utilizing the services of recruitment professionals, it is critically important to present yourself in a way that invites assistance. Headhunters, like everyone else in today's business world, have kept pace technologically. Most search firms are computerized and rely heavily on databases to store and retrieve information. What most job-changing professionals are unaware of, and what few recruiters explain, is *how* these systems actually work and *how* a candidate can and should fit in. But, before getting into the *hows*, let's first look at *why* these systems remain so secretive.

"A computer terminal is not some
clunky old television with a typewriter
in front of it. It is an interface where the
mind and body can connect with the
universe and move bits of it about."
—DOUGLAS ADAMS,
AUTHOR OF THE HITCHHIKER'S GUIDE TO THE GALAXY

CHAPTER 16

Byte Me!

One reason for the secrecy is the recruiter's concern that the candidate might feel like just another number in that recruiter's computer (0 or 1, in digital terms). Secondly, headhunters simply don't have time to explain all this so you will understand. Many people are resistant to what they perceive as an impersonal world of computerized information. They turn up their noses defiantly if they think they won't be "treated like a real person." Well, welcome to the 21st Century! I'm not saying that one shouldn't be treated well—that has nothing to do with *information storage and retrieval*. How you are treated and how your information is maintained are two separate issues. Regarding treatment, refer to Part II, Choosing a Recruiter. To understand how you are—and *must* be—stored, read on.

Let's face it: your **entire life** is literally held in so many bytes of computer language all over the world. From the phone company to your credit cards, even to your church, computerized databases are what keeps today's world "clicking". So, why not learn exactly how the systems work so you can work with them? Realize that any headhunter who whiles away hours on the phone making you feel "special," when they don't even have a position to tell you about, is probably either: 1) a novice, 2) not computerized, or 3) not working on a large enough scale to have much to offer you. Stay away from them!

I don't advocate that a recruiter not spend time understanding a candidate's desires. This should be done with *everyone* who either fits, or could fit, current or future openings in the headhunter's niche. Yet a candidate can't expect lengthy conversations at every twist and turn of the recruiter's process unless they are discussing viable opportunities for the candidate to explore. If it's just plain chit-chat you need, get it from other folks.

The ability to listen is a major factor in choosing a headhunter. What they do with what they've heard or seen makes all the difference in their ability to serve you. As you recall, if you talk with a recruiter repeatedly about what you want but then keep hearing about opportunities that don't fit, he isn't listening—*or* has inefficient memory storage systems. If, however, you rarely hear from him, and when you do, it's with close matches to your desires, then you are dealing with a recruiter who remembers what you're looking for, but won't call until he has it. Work with him! What has him call with positions that interest you is his *memory and note-taking system*. In today's information overloaded world, human memory only goes so far. Therefore, a headhunter's memory must be expanded by the most efficient technology in the recruiting business—computerized, **keyword searchable** databases.

I have seen many new technologies hit the recruiting industry with great impact. From the early '80s rise of the fax machine as a staple in every office ("Can you fax me the resume?") to the late '80s advent of the personal computer, all have dramatically affected the search business. Initially, computers supported the use of filing cabinets. Candidates were recorded with basics (name, address, phone number) and "coded" by particular job descriptions (235 = Mechanical Engineer; SM/El = Sales Manager in Electronics; etc.) or duties (FS, BGT, CPA = a Certified Public Accountant with financial statements and budgeting experience). The computer merely *pointed* to where the hardcopy of a resume was stored. These first systems were life altering for the recruiting profession and helped it manage vast amounts of information much more efficiently.

However, ever-expanding technology has rendered early computer usage obsolete. Today, clients are highly specific about the exact experience of the candidates they want to see, so ever more precise data storage and retrieval are key to a professional recruiter's suc-

> "Every new change forces all companies in an industry to adapt their strategies to that change."
> —BILL GATES

cess. Computers have now *replaced* filing cabinets.

Resumes pour in by mail, fax, and e-mail, and it is crucial for recruiters to store as much detailed information as possible for easy, accurate retrieval. Early systems were limited in that the candidate's information was saved in a basic profile form that may or may not have included all the specifics such as actual products sold, software utilized, languages spoken, certifications and/or degrees. Even if these first databases did include all vital information, it was costly and time consuming to have each candidate entered into the system manually. Today's leading-edge software for the recruiting industry solves such problems and provides the ultimate in *specific* candidate information storage. Databases are now *keyword searchable*, allowing for a resume to be input as a whole into the computer, ready to be retrieved instantaneously based on an identified keyword.

Through **Optical Character Recognition (OCR)** technology, a computer can now read a resume and input it into the system in an easy-to-read text format. A mailed-in resume can be viewed by a *scanner* which takes a picture of the resume and then, through an internal vocabulary list, sorts out the lines forming the image into letters and words of text (called "scanning in" or "OCRing" a resume). Most faxed resumes today are actually received *on the computer* by one of many fax software packages on the market, enabling a recruiter to flip through his "in-box" of faxes to save or print only those of interest. These faxes are still only images on the screen and also get "OCR'd" into the computer and converted into text. E-mailed resumes are already in text form (need no OCRing) and are simply transferred into the database. Note: regardless of the arrival form of any relevant resume, it is destined to become a "text file" in a contemporary recruiter's database.

> "If anybody wants to keep creating they have to be about change."
>
> —MILES DAVIS

In the same way a computer can read a single resume and add it to a database, it can also read all the resumes in that database with the simple click of a mouse. This is where the term *keyword searchable* (KWS) comes in. A headhunter, trying to locate particular experience or attributes of candidates for her client, will tell the computer what specific, or "key," words or phrases to search for. The database then reads each resume in its memory with a fine-tooth comb, noting every instance in which those words or phrases appear. This is tantamount to having 5 or 6 people review every resume in a wall-full of file cabinets. And instead of 4 days, it generally takes the computer only minutes, or seconds, to complete the task. So, today's recruiter would be shamefully amiss not utilizing these cutting-edge, information-management tools.

The questions then arise: "If I want to utilize a contemporary headhunter, and I know that she is going to store my information in a bits-and-bytes fashion on the computer, how do I best present myself 1) in the easiest form possible to get into the database, and 2) in such a way that I can be 'retrieved' appropriately and stand out for her to notice?"

Now, *these* are intelligent questions. Far more advanced than "Do you have anything for me *now*? Otherwise, I won't send my resume." Remember, working with a modern recruiter is not just about being "treated like a real person," but simply an issue of being retrieved from the database, being noticed, and *then* being treated like a real person. Believe me, recruiters *want* to help you—that's how we make our living.

Help me
help you!

CHAPTER 17

Grease is Slicker Than Sandpaper

Try to create a smooth path for your information to get from your caring hands into the headhunter's system. It can mean the difference in your getting noticed and notified.

AS THE HEAD TURNS

Hedda's Office: Scene 7/Take 1

A C T I O N !

HEDDA HUNTER: "This is **Professional** Search. May I help you?"

H. R. KIDDING: "Well, I certainly hope so. As a matter of fact, I'm surprised that I am having to call you, long-distance and all. I sent my background information in over two months ago and I haven't heard a thing from your firm. With a Masters and Ph.D. in . . . "

HEDDA HUNTER: "[under breath] *whew . . . Thank God!* Well, sir, I'm sorry to hear that. We do have a rather efficient system here but, nonetheless, some things do fall through the cracks. Let me see if I can help you. Now, what is your name?"

H. R. Kidding:	"Hugh Kidding. That's H-U-G-H K-I-D-D-I-N-G."
Hedda Hunter:	"And just when, approximately, did you send it in?"
H. R. Kidding:	"I believe it was the first of April."
Hedda Hunter:	"O.K., let me look in my log here . . . You know, Mr. Kidding, you don't show up in our records. Again, sometimes things may slip through the cracks. How did you send it?"
H. R. Kidding:	"I can't believe you don't have it! I took the utmost care in folding the parchment perfectly into the bottle. The ancient Balinese text was written in indelible ink and I was certain of the direction of the trade winds. As an acclaimed professor of Archeology and Asian Society Specialist (A.S.S.), studying the history of the South Pacific headhunters, I thought my experience could be put to good use in your organization. You are headhunters, are you not?"
Hedda Hunter:	" . . . are you kidding?"
H. R. Kidding:	"No, Hugh R. Kidding."
Hedda Hunter:	"No, *I'm not* kidding! Who is this anyhow?"
H. R. Kidding:	"*Hugh R. Kid . . .* "
Hedda Hunter:	"*STOP! Just STOP!* What's happening to the world? Where have all the regular people gone? *AAAARRRRGGGGHHHH!!!!*"

— C U T ! —

Poor Hedda may have hunted her last head, or lost hers, but the point is critical: hearing about career opportunities quickly means your resume must be well greased when sent to a recruiter—in a form creating the least *resistance* to, and thereby sliding best into, the database. By "resistance" I mean the time, labor, and attention required to translate your resume into KWS database form. Without a really hot position that you would fit *immediately*, rarely will a head-hunter take the time, with the onslaught of resumes pouring in, to call you and request that you re-send your resume in a better form. This is especially true if you are a marginally placeable candidate (less placeable based on specialty, background, etc.). However, resumes presented in the form of *least resistance*, even if marginally useful, will often make it into the database simply because they are so easy to include—just in case something for those people arises. Always consider this *resistance* factor in presenting your information to a recruiter: lower resistance = quicker potential results.

By far, **e-mail** is the best form of resume submission. Already in text form, it slips right into a database without a blink. The problem with *only* e-mailing is that e-mailed resumes often lose their shape. Recruiters want a form that goes into the database easily, but they also need a nice-looking, presentable version to show their clients. Therefore, a headhunter wants a nice hardcopy of your resume *in addition* to having it in the database. It's good, if possible, to provide both forms: an easily transferable one, and a nice-looking one. Simply attach a separate "file" of your resume, formatted, say, in Microsoft Word (Word), to your e-mailed text version which can then be printed and held as a nice hardcopy.

> "Whoever desires constant success must change his conduct with the times."
> —MACHIAVELLI

There's another reason to e-mail your information both ways, standard text e-mail and in an attachment. E-mailing *only* an attached file, with no actual resume visible, creates a lag because the recruiter has to open the file just to get a sense of what you are about. When poring through e-mails, he would rather not keep switching between his browser and another program to open the attachment. Rather than view an attached file immediately, he will save it to his computer's hard drive to view later, so as not to interrupt the flow getting through all those e-mails. Unfortunately for you, the candidate, this means a delay in getting your resume seen. To be noticed as quickly as possible, the ideal form of resume submission is, again, to have it contained within the body of the e-mail for immediate perusal as well as in an attached file at the bottom of the same e-mail for clean, hardcopy purposes. (Note: remember this when signing up with resume "blasting"services—investigate their end product.) This way, a recruiter can tell immediately if you are someone to get into his database and can save your information appropriately. If you fit anything currently hot on his desk, he has a nice hardcopy to use right away. (See Example 4.1 as an illustration, and Appendix B for detailed instructions on designing your e-mail this way.)

A few facts about e-mailing:

- E-mail the resume itself. Don't send a headhunter searching for it by simply referencing your Web site or otherwise "posted" resume—lay it out clearly for her. The Web version often won't print well, needs a password for access, or is just too "cute" to use effectively. When candidates refer me to their resume elsewhere, invariably I e-mail them a reply requesting a direct submission. This adds more time to your information being seen by the recruiter and getting into the database.
- When responding to a recruiter-posted opportunity on the Internet, refer to the *position title* in your e-mail, fax, or letter, not a job ID number (which is often randomly assigned by the posting site, not the recruiter). State the specific job title you are applying for, even if the site's e-mail reply automatically includes the ID number.
- Make sure your resume and cover letter list your own personal/home e-mail address so you can always be

contacted regardless of changes in employer or residence.

- Because e-mail can get warped, stretched, and word-wrapped in the sending process—and an "attached" file can often, inadvertently, not get attached—it's always a good idea to test your e-mail to see if what you are sending out has any problems. E-mail yourself: you won't go blind!

The following example provides a starting point for our discussion of efficient and effective resume submission to recruiters.

Example 4.1

Subject: Resume Submission
Date: Mon, 18 Oct 1999 12:47:23 PDT
From: "MajorLeverBose" <loquacious@anymail.com>
To: aps@apscareersearch.com
Two Word attachments also included
****

Dear Mr. Gurney,

I am writing to express interest in the Senior VP/Director of Technology position I saw posted on thisjobs4U.com. I am extremely motivated to apply my many years of applicable experience in a setting such as the one described.

I am also open to other senior-level Information Technology positions that you may come across, as long as there is a focus on implementation of new systems as opposed to simply maintenance. Integration of cutting-edge technologies is my forte. I am well seasoned in the financial services industry but am open to hear of opportunities outside of that realm.

On leaving the military in 1996, I married and moved to the Northwest. For the following two years, I played an instrumental role in the development of Safe Bank's corporate call centers and education department. When the corporate CEO left in 1998 to spearhead the start-up of Some Bank Credit Services, I was invited to join him in a senior IT capacity. I was one of the original 12 managers starting the company. Now, with our recent acquisition by Yet Another Bank, I perceive an overlap in my duties and, therefore, am beginning a job search.

My current compensation is $90K, including bonus. I would like to hear about positions starting at no less than $100K. Though my preference is to remain in Portland, I will entertain all West Coast opportunities.

Please keep my information on file and thank you for your consideration.

Sincerely,

Major Lever Bose

* * * * * * * * * * * * * * * * * RESUME* * * * * * * * * * * * * * * * *

Maj. Lever Bose
Vice President and Business Integration Manager (MIS/IT)
1412 Raintree Lane
Portland, Oregon 97201
(503) 236-7575, fax (503) 243-7600
Internet: loquacious@anymail.com

Objective: Seeking a position which will utilize my expertise in technology management, employee training and development, business integration, communications, strategic planning, and team leadership.

Accomplishments:
* Broad experience in managing a variety of professionals in technology, training and development, communications and quality control
* Extensive call center experience emphasizing technology integration, business integration, negotiation, employee development and facilities management

* Highly developed writing, public speaking, presentation and sales skills
* From startup, managed and planned the development of data and telephony integration to support 420 workstations
* Strategic planning for disaster recovery from local to wide area for telephony and business resumption
* Directed enterprise-wide connectivity with third party and business affiliates
* Negotiated multiple contracts with various vendors
* Experienced in project management and in initiating large group trainings for migration to new technologies, software upgrades, acquisitions, mergers and widespread operational/policy changes
* Wrote operational policies involving significant user and customer input

Relevant Experience:

Jan 1998 - Present
   Some Bank Credit Services (subsidiary of Yet Another Bank)
   Portland, Oregon
   Vice President, Manager IT / Business Integration
   Responsible for technology operations and implementations for a high-volume call center with specific emphasis on financial and business impact. Managed all staff and projects in the following areas: Data Networking, Technology Integration, Quality, Desktop Applications, Telecommunications, Training and Development, Consultant Relationships, Help Desk, Communications and Facilities.
   Directed all vendor relationships while implementing new technology, training, facilities and associated contracts. Redesigned Training and Development to meet the needs of both new hires and tenured employees. Wrote job descriptions

and performed all functions of personnel management including coaching, counseling and corrective action. Managed corporate Intranet creation, content and future development.

1996 - Jan 1998

Safe Bank, US Customer Service

Portland, Oregon

Officer, Training and Development /Communications Manager

Responsible for new hire and current employee training and development for Safe Bank's call centers in Portland, Oregon, and Boise, Idaho. Implemented, coordinated, and administered programs consistent with the organization's goals and objectives. Supervised 11 direct reports consisting of Training Specialists and Communication Representatives with a budget of approximately 450K. Worked closely with Corporate Education to implement and monitor appropriate training programs to support identified core skill requirements.

Managed development and design of courses and associated materials including Multimedia/CBT training design. Involved in policy creation, employee performance evaluations, as well as coaching, counseling and corrective action.

1992-1996

Systems Engineer

U.S. Army Information Systems Command

Vienna, Virginia

Designed, installed and integrated secure networks for top-secret information systems. Functioned as senior technical advisor and project manager for worldwide turnkey installations. Also served as top QA/QC & Physical Security inspector for all locations within my division. Supervised and managed installation teams. Completed all projects ahead of schedule and received "Outstanding" rating by superiors. Received Army Meritorious Service and Achievement Medals.

Education:

M. S., Computer Engineering, Syracuse University, Syracuse, New York

Graduation Project and Paper: "Computer and Network Security —Intrusion Detection Systems"

United States Army Management Engineering Training Agency, Rock Island, Illinois

Quality and Reliability Engineering - Graduate

B.S.E., Aerospace Engineering, University of Michigan, Ann Arbor, Michigan

Additional Education and Workshops:

Successful Training Management, Behavioral Description Interviewing, Training Needs Analysis, Coaching, Counseling & Corrective Action (Workshop), Designing Computer Based Training, Human Resource Management (Workshop), Designing Web Pages, Personnel and the Law, Photoshop 1 & 2 (Workshop), Law and Banking, Visual Basic 1 & 2 (Workshop), Speech Team

Software and Equipment:

Microsoft Word, Excel, PowerPoint, Director for Windows 5.0, Microsoft Project; Photoshop 4.0; Extreme 3D 1.0; Langevin Design-ware (Course Development Software); Maximizer Data Base (Client Contact); Sound Designer; NetObjects 2.0; Q-sheet; Vision; Back Stage; Windows NT, WIN95, WIN98; Secure/non-secure networks; Video teleconferencing, fiber optics and paging; Satellite & Microwave Radios (HF/UHF/VHF/SHF); FCC 2048, IDNX and SPX Mux; CISCO and Newbridge routers; Voice and E-mail servers; PBX Switch; Inmarsat; LAN/ WAN.

AFFILIATIONS: Professional and philanthropic affiliations with the Ovaltine Chamber of Commerce, YMCA of Oregon, and Friends of the Trees.

REFERENCES: Available upon request

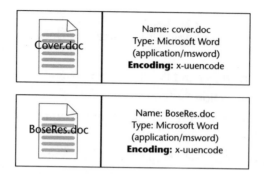

	Name: cover.doc
Cover.doc	Type: Microsoft Word (application/msword) **Encoding:** x-uuencode

	Name: BoseRes.doc
BoseRes.doc	Type: Microsoft Word (application/msword) **Encoding:** x-uuencode

(*Note: attached Word files of the same cover letter and resume*)

Major Bose's information, presented via e-mail, plops into the database immediately. You may accuse him of being too wordy, but you can't fault him for omitting anything! (See Appendix A for a critique of the Major's resume.) This type of intricate detail, with a full serving of *keywords* for the computer to search, renders him highly retrievable in a database search for a relevant position. Therefore, he will hear about more opportunities than a candidate without such detail.

After e-mail, the next best way to submit yourself to a recruiter is to **fax** your resume. If the headhunter has a computerized fax retrieval system (e.g., Winfax), the resume arrives on a computer screen, not paper, and can be OCR'd by a software which translates the faxed image into letters and words of text for database purposes. There is, however, 2-way resistance here. First, the OCR phase takes time (1-4 minutes). Second, though OCR software has grown stronger in deciphering resumes based on improved, internal "vocabulary" systems, they remain imperfect. This means that an OCR'd resume must be "proofed" afterwards so that any misspellings or errors are corrected before it is saved in the database (4-6 minutes). A word to the wise: a database is only able to search out *correctly spelled* keywords.

Garbage In—Garbage Out!

All told, converting a fax received on computer into useable, accurate, KWS database form requires from 5-10 minutes of translation. This may sound minimal, and the least a headhunter could invest in you—given the quintessential candidate that you are—but when you multiply it by all the resumes received from other quintessential candidates, it adds up.

If your headhunter recipient does *not* have a computerized fax retrieval system, then he probably doesn't even have a computer. He is working from resumes that spit out of a fax machine, often faded, lacking in definition, and sometimes on slick, flimsy paper. No database resistance here—because there's no database! This type of recruiting operation still exists, and such outdated equipment suggests less opportunity for long-term success with a recruiter.

There is one saving grace to faxing: it can give a recruiter an immediate, nice-looking hardcopy for her files. She simply prints out what she sees on her screen. However, a faxed resume *never* looks as clean or presentable as a digital version (e.g., Word file)—it becomes a "third generation" (faxed twice) document when sent out by the recruiter to a client: *doable*, but not the best first impression for your resume.

To summarize, though faxed-in resume submissions are preferable to the last and worst alternative—*mail*—they nonetheless create significant database resistance. If faxing is your only option, you can make your faxed-in resume "OCR Friendly." What will determine whether or not this method will land you in the database quickly is the recruiter's computerized fax retrieval and OCR software—or lack thereof.

Fax Friendly Guidelines

1. **Font:** standard Times New Roman. 11 or 12 point. 10 point on a faxed resume, combined with poor fax

quality, may mean the recruiter has to do much more correcting because the OCR software can't read it well.

2. **Margins:** top/bottom = ¾ inch; side = 1 inch. Smaller margins create "word wrap" when transferring into a database. ***Left-Justify Everything!*** Large indentations following stacked headings (e.g., PROFESSIONAL EXPERIENCE:, ACCOMPLISHMENTS:, EDUCATION:, etc.), often used by those with light experience so as to fill the page, warp the OCR software's ability to comprehend—requiring more correction. Try to separate ideas horizontally rather than in vertical, widely-spaced columns.

3. **Italics:** best to just stay away from them unless e-mailing—OCR software doesn't like them and can't read them correctly.

4. **All Caps:** on the Internet, this is considered "shouting." No need for that in resumes. It's annoying, and OCR software doesn't dig it.

(Example 4.2 on page 131 illustrates an unfriendly resume, but 4.3 is quite workable)

Finally, let's discuss the deadliest form of resume submission. If you want to ensure that your resume *never* gets into the recruiter's database or, if it does, probably weeks after submission, be sure to **mail** it. Why? People have mailed resumes throughout history—at least since the Pony Express, right? Right! But *that's history* and it simply doesn't work in today's computerized recruiting world. Remember, the primary *files* and *folders* used in offices today are comprised of bits and bytes in a computer, not steel or paper. Given that you want to be using a contemporary recruiter, don't send your resume in an archaic form. A mailed-in resume only gets into the database by being scanned-in, which takes 10-15 minutes to process. So it shouldn't surprise you that they often get put to the side for a while . . . a long while. Of course, if your resume is *exactly* what the doctor ordered for that headhunter, he may call you to discuss it and ask you to resubmit by fax or e-mail. Don't count on being such a perfect fit. Just concentrate on getting into the database and, therefore, stay away from this most resistant form of resume submission at all costs.

> "Change is the law of life. And those who look only to the past or present are certain to miss the future."
>
> —JOHN F. KENNEDY

The point of all this is simply to give you an insider's perspective on how information flows best into today's recruiting offices. You lose nothing by focusing on the least-resistant forms of submission because, again, if a recruiter cannot be e-mailed, she may not be contemporary enough to advance your best interests.

Database Resistance

E-mailed resume with attached-file version	Least
E-mailed resume	
Faxed-in resume (with computerized retrieval)	↓
Mailed-in resume	Most

CHAPTER 18

A Loaded Gun is Best for Hunting

Now we come to the most significant factor in your chance of hearing about that "perfect job." Whether you want to elevate yourself along a chosen career path in which you already have experience or find something different, how you construct and *load* your resume is critical to your retrievability from the database when a recruiter has the right position for you. I've devoted Appendix A to the subject of resume styles that recruiters prefer—the design aspect. Let's talk now about content. For your resume to be retrieved in a database keyword search, *the keywords must be present.*

Example: a headhunter is searching his system to isolate appropriate candidates for a hot, new sales position requiring a candidate with 5 years experience in business-to-business sales of telephone- or software-related services. Based on the client's criteria, the candidate must have been a top performer among sales peers, with rankings/awards to prove it, and must have at least a Bachelor's degree. There are certain *keywords* the recruiter will input in a certain way to search the database for all possible matches:

(sales OR sold OR sell)

AND

[phone OR (long AND distance)
OR bell OR sprint OR mci
OR wireless OR software]

AND

(bachelor OR b.s. OR b.a. OR b.b.a.
OR degree OR g.p.a.
OR university OR college)

AND

(quota OR award
OR club OR rank)

With this criteria in mind, examine the following two resumes . . . which do you think will come up in that recruiter's search?

Example 4.2

Manny O. Namischen
1448 Beach Street, #226
Los Angeles, CA 90292
(310) 555-1212

OBJECTIVE: To pursue a career in a hi-tech industry with opportunity for growth and development.

PROFESSIONAL EXPERIENCE:

8/94 - Present

MA BELL WIRELESS
Los Angeles, CA
Senior Account Executive
- Responsible for opening new accounts and managing existing accounts
- Cold calling, canvassing, and prospecting to build client base
- Products included entire line of cellular paging equipment and related services
- Consistent top performer, attaining President's Club for each year of employment

5/92 - 8/94

SURPRISE RENT-A-CAR
Austin, TX
Assistant Branch Manager
Supervised nine employees and was responsible for:
- Training new employees
- Assisting staff with customer service and employee concerns
- Developing and maintaining relationships with contracted vendors
- Handling accounts receivable and payable
- Increasing fleet by 25% as an Assistant Manager at three locations

ACCOMPLISHMENTS/ AFFILIATIONS:

Volunteers of America, Donations Coordinator, San Fernando, CA
Most valuable player, UT Football Junior Varsity, 1991
Vice President, Alpha Chi Omega, 1990-91

COMPUTER SKILLS: Microsoft Office 95, ACT Contact Manager

EDUCATION: University of Texas, Austin
B.S. Business Administration, 1992

PROFESSIONAL REFERENCES: Available upon request

Example 4.3

Pat Peeves
23 Knob Hill, Apt. 103
San Francisco, CA 94115
Ph: (415) 936-1212
Fax: (415) 557-4400
ideosinc@junkmail.com

Professional Experience:
Dynamic Software Corporation   4/96 - Present
San Francisco, CA
Account Manager
- Sold enhanced Internet communications software to Fortune 500 accounts. Clients included Dole, Bechtel, Wells Fargo, Kaiser Permanente.
- Opened a new sales territory in Northern California allowing for focused account management with more than 20 key customers.
- Consistently exceed quota by 25-30%.
- Delivered effective sales presentations to business groups and individuals within the sales organization promoting products and services.
- Consultative sales approach includes defining business problems and objectives, analyzing current processes, and uncovering high pay-off training opportunities.

Dupes Worldwide   6/93 - 4/96
San Francisco, CA
Account Representative
- Sold copier systems within local territory of San Francisco.
- Responsibilities included generating prospects by cold-calling and maintaining customer base; developing and negotiating competitive proposals; consulting potential customers on implementing most effective and productive office automation solutions.
- Called on my assigned geographical territory of professional businesses including large financial organizations, insurance companies, law firms, local and international banks.
- Exceeded company quota by 120% in February and March 1996.
- Won "Representative-of-the-Office" in March 1996.

Technical Skills:
Proficient in Microsoft Word, Microsoft Excel; Internet related software such as mail clients, browsers, and streaming media; working knowledge of Dynamic Internet solutions software and commerce packages.

Education:
Bachelor of Science, Marketing, University of California, Berkeley, 1992

Seminars/Courses:
Strategic Selling - Miller - Heiman
Effective Communications - American Management Association
Public Speaking - Dale Carnegie

References: Available upon request

Notice that Manny Namischen is clearly an appropriate sales candidate to consider for this position, yet as the recruiter's search is constructed, *his resume will not come up!* The word "sales" or any derivation thereof is nowhere to be found in his resume. The recruiter may be wise enough to search for the word "account" as well, or may even take "sales" out as a search criteria. However, *you don't want to be second-guessing exactly how the recruiter is going to design a search.* You want to be a big enough fish to be caught by any size net appropriate to either your background or aspirations. So, it is critical to construct and load your resume with those words, and *only* those words, which are *key* to that background and those aspirations.

A point regarding cover letters: as a resume generally covers your past, a cover letter can point the way to your future. Anything substantial mentioned in a cover letter is often included with your resume in the database, so be certain to include the keywords of your objectives and aspirations, just as in your resume you included the keywords of your background. This way, both your past and future wishes can be searched.

*Resumes allow your past to be searched;
cover letters allow your future*

In the old days, before the advent of such tremendous information management technologies as KWS databases, one could count on a certain amount of information being assumed or *read into* a resume because they were sorted and reviewed by hand and eye during a file search. Therefore, Manny Namischen's resume would obviously stand out as a sales candidate. But now, at least for retrieval purposes, *the computer* reads the resume. Although artificial intelligence has come a long way ... databases can't *assume.*

It can't find
what you ain't writ down!

It is imperative that both your resume and cover letter contain every single word or phrase that could serve to identify you with the types of positions you've had or would like to have. No need to go overboard with words like "woman," "work," and "get paid," but words which characterize specific skills, traits, products, degrees, work environments, titles, and technical and industry-specific terms are highly searchable.

If you dabble on the Internet, you know a bit about how "search engines" work. When web pages are designed, they are coded with keywords that bring Web surfers to that page when exploring a particular subject. Commerce on the web has grown tremendously as more and more businesses are marketing themselves through Web sites. For example, typing "recruiters" into a search engine will literally direct you to thousands of recruiter Web sites. It's the same with a headhunter's KWS database. You, just like a business on the web, want to *market* yourself to that recruiter every time he searches his database for candidates with your specialty, experience, and interests.

A weak load means a bumpy road
To finding the right job for you;
Make it easier to find—
Keep the database in mind
When you list "have done" and "will do"

The question then becomes: "What *keywords* do I specifically need to build into my resume so I'll 'pop up' for that headhunter conducting a database search to fill my perfect job?"

Good question. First, do an inventory of the positions you've listed to see where, in your resume, you are assuming that the reader understands something not stated specifically. Here are some important areas to consider:

1. FUNCTION/SKILLS/RESPONSIBILITIES

     Example 4.2 above shows the importance of expressing your job function clearly. In addition to titles (preferably *not* abbreviated), include the main responsibilities carried out in that function. For example, in the world of sales, an oft-used hiring criteria for certain positions is the ability to "cold-call," "canvass" or "prospect" for new accounts. So, a sales representative with these skills, seeking to utilize them in their next position, would most certainly include them: they are KWS.

     Another example: you are a financial analyst and your past experience does not include work in Securities and Exchange Commission (SEC) or 10-K reporting, but you want to move into this area. In your cover letter, be sure to state these skills as areas of interest:

     My intention is to secure a growth-oriented position as a Senior Financial Analyst with a focus on SEC and 10-K reporting

The point is to leave no stone unturned in ensuring that all words *key* to your primary functions and duties, or desired functions and duties, are included in the body of your resume and cover letter.

2. **JOB-SPECIFIC TERMS OR PHRASES (BUZZWORDS)**

Often there are words and phrases specific to a particular field. To the depth that a headhunter's client requires her to go in search of the "perfect candidate," these words and phrases can become KWS targets. For instance, one of my clients seeking to fill 3 Human Resource Manager positions around the country required that a candidate have hands-on experience dealing with "cultural change" and "change management." Therefore, these phrases became search criteria and, to my amazement when conducting a keyword search, many candidates had those specific phrases in the body of their resume. Another example would be a salesperson with "business-to-business" and/or "one-call close" sales experience. These phrases could also be targets for a keyword search.

In technical fields, it is vitally important that *every* technical term, process, certification, or knowledge be stated specifically. Interestingly, technical candidates, be they engineering-, programming-, or systems-related, are often the best at spelling out these KWS targets. One caution, however, when abbreviating technical terms or phrases: a good rule of thumb is to both spell out *and* abbreviate those that you have seen spelled out before. If you have *never* seen an acronym or abbreviation spelled out, then just include the acronym or abbreviation without spelling it out. For example, for professionals in manufacturing, **JIT** is a process for "just-in-time" delivery of raw materials. This phrase is seen both abbreviated and spelled out, so do both in your resume. However, the acronym **OSHA**

(Occupational Safety and Health Administration) is hardly ever spelled out, so neither would you.

3. SPECIFIC PRODUCTS/SERVICES

I can't tell you how many resumes come into my office from seemingly strong candidates with stable work histories but without indication of the products or services with which they have been involved. Most recruiters' clients want candidates who already have experience with similar products or services. Therefore, this is an important KWS criteria in conducting a database search. Often, especially in a "functional" resume, specific areas of responsibility or duties are outlined for 90% of a person's resume, leaving only a few lines to state dates and places of employment. Beware: *most company names say nothing about their particular line of work.* "**ABC Company**" does not tell me whether they produce or sell widgets or wigs. So, it is vitally important to spell out the types of products or services your employers and you, specifically, have dealt with. Be careful not to assume that the reader understands anything not stated: though "**Gerber Foods**" conjures up an immediate association of baby food on my child's face, the floor, and my shirt, my childless computer can't assume anything. State "baby food" clearly on your resume.

4. INDUSTRY OR WORK ENVIRONMENT

The computer also can't distinguish which *field* you are in by the name of your employer. "**Sony Pictures**" does not say you are in the "entertainment" industry, and a specific industry is always a KWS target. Also, if your past employers have been "manufacturing" companies or you have been involved in "industrial" or "international" sales, then you want those KWS words to be in the body of your resume.

When in Doubt,
Spell it Out!

These are only a few main areas to be specific about. Other KWS targets would be degrees, certifications, geographic locations, and even awards. Remember, though your resume and cover letter will be seen *initially* by recruiters to determine whether or not you should go into the database, the only way they will see it *again* is if it's *fully loaded* with all the words and phrases that point the way to the perfect position for you. (See Appendix A for more details on resume and keyword design.)

> "Keep your resume locked, loaded, and ready to fire at all times . . . "
> —HARVEY MACKAY,
> SHARKPROOF

When incorporating keywords into your resume, loading does not mean lengthening. In fact, there's rarely a reason to go beyond one page, with the exception of some hi-tech candidates (Maj. Lever Bose above—but even *he* is long-winded) who must spell out tons of technical experience and systems/software used. Most other job seekers can fit necessary information into a one-page resume. More length to a resume means more resistance getting it into the database (more time to process, correct, etc.). A resume can be fully loaded without adding length: simply add specifics. And, never take the easy way out by putting a huge block of keywords at the top of your resume in web-page fashion. In addition to being unattractive and taking crucial space from the body of the resume, it's difficult for the recruiter who pulls it up in the database to comprehend. You want it loaded with information, but still attractive and "reader friendly."

The *content* of a resume is important, but humans read contextually. Build your KWS targets into the *context* of the resume and the *structure* of your descriptive sentences so a recruiter can see how the term or phrase she was searching for relates to your background. Contextual loading gives more punch and substance to the resume. If you have performed keyword searches on the Internet, you know how frustrating it is to pull up a document that lists a block of keywords not necessarily germane to that document. So, keep the KWS target words and phrases inside the descriptive body of the resume. EXCEPTION: summaries of software, systems, or job-skills utilized may all be listed as a group separate from the rest of the resume. Example 4.4 illustrates a proper, contextually loaded resume.

Example 4.4

Ima Goodun
1313 Mockingbird Lane
Banksville, Ohio 45331
H: (419) 936-1212   W: (419) 259-5202   Pg: (419) 243-4446
numbersgal@openmail.com

Objective: Seeking a position in economic analysis, financial analysis, or a related position leveraging my experience in Financial Services and background in Economics.

Summary: Substantive experience in Financial Services; firm understanding of financial and investment markets; credit and industry analysis, cash flow projections, modeling; SAS; Excel.

Professional Experience:

Money Mutual, Inc.   1/97 - Present
(formerly Humma Humma Bank)
Banksville, OH
Senior Accountant
- Selected as a member of merger transition team that prepared necessary reports to comply with SEC and regulatory requirements for merger of MMI and HHB.
- Analyzed financial data, prepared Securities and Exchange Commission (SEC) 10-K and 10-Q reports of parent and subsidiaries with $103 billion in assets.
- Performed monthly closings and prepared financial reports for Board of Directors.

Preferential Securities   6/93 - 12/96
Moolah Township, CT
Project Analyst, Financial Planning and Analysis Department
- Conducted cost/benefit analysis for clients' strategic options; cash flow projections and modeling; credit, industry and sensitivity analysis.
- Analyzed and reviewed stock indenture debt-service characteristics; created debt service and trade schedules.
- Generated accurate and timely prospectuses to determine and enforce compliance with stringent stock targets.
- Processed and recorded trades, expenses, and dividends to an automated accounting system.
- Monitored settlement of domestic securities to ensure proper end-of-day dollar positions.

Education:
M.B.A., emphasis in Accounting, 1996
University of California, Los Angeles
G.P.A. 3.6/4.0
B.A. in Economics, 1992
Clemson University, Clemson, SC
G.P.A. 3.8/4.0 Dean's List

CHAPTER 19

Cover Yourself!

I've already mentioned the importance of including words and phrases relevant to the change you are seeking in your cover letter. A good, informative cover letter, chock-full of specifics, will often be included in the database with your resume. Even if you are an accountant with no sales experience but wanting to move into, say, software sales, a cover letter with those keywords could at least get you *seen* in a database search by a headhunter—especially if she has a client in the field of accounting software who is willing to take a beginning salesperson. The point is to load the cover letter just as you would the resume.

Now here comes a harsh reality. There's something you should know about cover letters. For the most part, they are **not read** when initially received but flipped over to the resume. A recruiter is more focused on the resume because he can often tell with one quick flash whether a candidate falls into his specialty. Personally, the time I spend on a resume that falls outside of my specialties can be as short as 3-5 seconds, with literally no time for the attached cover letter.

Call it cruel and short sighted, but that's the way it works in recruitment offices. Headhunters must stay focused on helping those people we *know* we can help (in our field, specialties, etc.). Recruiters are already fixated on certain clients and positions they are trying to fill—their eyes almost filter everything else out. They can tell just by the resume, without glancing at the cover letter, whether or not you can satisfy their immediate need.

So, don't break your neck over a cover letter to a headhunter. Except for some quick and necessary basics, cover letters get little attention. I don't know if Human Resource departments at hiring companies actually spend time reading them. I seriously doubt it: HR departments are also focused on specific positions to fill, and they have even *less* time to deal with incoming resumes. Send a cover letter, yes, and include certain vital information, but don't worry about giving your life story or an analytical interpretation of your background—it just won't matter. If, in fact, you *are* someone in whom the recruiter has an interest (determined quickly by your resume), you will get a call for the life story.

Here's why you *do* want to include a simple cover letter. Aren't you tired of meeting or getting calls from recruiters who inquire into your particulars but never call with an opportunity? Save yourself a lot of time by providing the minimal information a headhunter usually wants to know *up-front* in the cover letter. That way, she can't play dumb and call you about a $50,000 position when you stated your minimum salary requirement was $70,000. Or, if she does, you can quickly assess how good a listener she is.

The basics of a good cover letter:

1. **All Contact Information.** Just to be safe. If you fax, sometimes every page won't come through, so list name, address, all contact numbers, and e-mail address on the cover.

2. **Reasons for Leaving.** Describe briefly why you're on the market and, in a short sentence for each position, why you've moved in the past. This is especially important for a resume that smells of rubber (lots of bouncing around). To possibly attract a recruiter, you'd better strike preemptively with a good reason for moving before you strike out. But keep it short!

3. **Positions and Industries of Interest.** Actually spell out the titles and industries for which you would like to be considered.

4. **Salary History and Expectations.** It doesn't matter that you are "flexible" or "open on compensation commensurate with duties and responsibilities"—*you do have a **bottom** line.* Not that a recruiter is going to focus on your bottom line (remember, the more *you* make, the more *we* make), but he has to know your range of consideration. Regardless of how much you don't want your last compensation to impact your next, 99% of the time it does. Deal with it! Employers generally offer at least *some* increase over your last salary, and a recruiter can negotiate for as much possible, but the company isn't going to give you a 50% raise! Simply spell out what you've earned in each of your positions so that the headhunter can see your progression, and state a salary range you're willing to consider.

AS THE HEAD TURNS

H.R. Department: Scene 8/Take 1

A C T I O N !

Reaching the end of a job interview, the Human Resources person asked the young Engineer fresh out of MIT . . .

C. NITALL: "What starting salary were you looking for?"

YUNG N. BRAZEN: "In the neighborhood of $125,000 a year, depending on the benefits package."

C. NITALL: "Well, what would you say to a package of 5-weeks vacation, 14 paid holidays, full medical and dental, company-matching retirement fund to 50% of salary, and a company car leased every 2 years—say, a red Corvette?"

YUNG N. BRAZEN: "Wow! Are you kidding?"

C. NITALL: "Yeah, but you started it."

— C U T ! —

5. **Locations of Interest.** State either that you want to stay within a certain locale (city, state) or spell out exactly which cities, states, or regions of the country/world you would consider. This KWS information can be extremely valuable in a database search, especially for recruiters who serve nationwide or worldwide clients.

Example 4.5 demonstrates a simple, adequate cover letter. This basic information, loaded with keywords of a desired change, gives the recruiter quick answers to frequently asked questions without having to get on the phone and bother you.

Example 4.5

Ima Goodun
1313 Mockingbird Lane
Banksville, OH 45331

Dear Mr. Gurney:

As you requested, I am enclosing my resume for consideration for a **sales/investment broker** or **trading** position with a banking or investment institution. Because of my background in financial analysis and investment banking, I believe my technical skills would enhance my ability to provide quality investment solutions to prospective clients. I have gained a reputation for working well with people, communicating options clearly, and selling clients on profitable solutions.

Salary history:
Money Mutual	
Beginning salary	$48,000 plus 10% bonus
Current salary	$52,500 (no bonus due to merger)
Preferential Securities	
Beginning Salary	$36,000 plus 15% bonus
Ending Salary	$42,000 plus 12% bonus

I am interested in hearing about positions that start at a $45-50K base with training and growth opportunities. Should I need to start at a lower base, if commission potential would bring my total first year income to between $65 and 70K, please call me. I prefer relocating to the Los Angeles area; however, for an attractive opportunity, I will consider anywhere in the West or Southwest.

Thank you for your consideration.
Sincerely,
Ima Goodun
H:(419) 936-1212
W:(419) 259-5202
Pg:(419) 243-4446
numbersgal@openmail.com

CHAPTER 16: Byte Me!

- ✔ Your information must and will be electronically stored in today's recruiting world
- ✔ Keyword searchable (KWS) databases are the memory of contemporary search firms

CHAPTER 17: Grease is Slicker Than Sandpaper

- ✔ Create the least database resistance when submitting your information
- ✔ E-mailing your resume, with (not only *as*) an attached file, is the preferred form of submission
- ✔ State the position title you are applying for
- ✔ Include your personal e-mail address and basic cover letter info
- ✔ Send it to yourself to check for problems
- ✔ If you must fax, follow the Fax Friendly Guidelines (p. 125–26)
- ✔ Don't mail your resume!

CHAPTER 18: A Loaded Gun is Best for Hunting

- ✔ How you load your resume determines your retrievability during a recruiter's database search
- ✔ Include all words related to your background and aspirations *contextually* in both the resume and cover letter
- ✔ Specifically load your resume with:
  - ❑ Function/skills/responsibilities
  - ❑ Job-specific terms or phrases (buzzwords)
  - ❑ Specific products/services
  - ❑ Industry or work environment

CHAPTER 19: Cover Yourself!

- ✔ Cover letters are generally not read in-depth, so don't write a novel
- ✔ Basic and vital information should include:
  - ❑ All contact information
  - ❑ Reasons for leaving
  - ❑ Positions and industries of interest
  - ❑ Salary history and expectations
  - ❑ Locations of interest

Afterword

I truly hope this book has given you a greater understanding and appreciation of headhunters. If it only helped you discriminate among them and get the most from their services, it has served its purpose. It is a career's worth of information from the perspective of one recruiter, but doesn't assume to be the last word on recruiting. There are thousands of outstanding professionals in the search industry, each with unique qualities and attributes. The guidance herein holds water in general, but may not always in specifics. For instance, an individual could be an exceptional recruiter, but the letters "CPC" or "CSAM" don't follow their name. Or, someone may be the nation's top headhunter in placing Pharmaceutical Sales Reps, but without benefit of a computer. Use the information as a set of guidelines rather than hard and fast dictums. Get to know your particular headhunters for their specific merits—or demerits—and let the value of those relationships be determined case by case. It's really their ability to produce results—to get you great interviews and positions—over the long term that matters.

> "There is no ultimate theory of the universe, just an infinite sequence of theories that describe the universe more and more accurately."
> —Stephen Hawking, scientist and best-selling author

Also take note that most of the advice on choosing recruiters in the "interview the interviewer" scenarios is directed toward the top, most marketable candidates in any field—the ones for whom recruiters jump through hoops. Not to say the points aren't food for thought for the marginally placeable candidate, but there may be less "weight" to throw around to get answers. Be bold, but practical—don't use more *vim* than you've got *vigor* to back up, lest you turn off a headhunter who figures that you're just not worth the interrogation.

I welcome your feedback through the publisher on ways to enhance this book, and wish you Happy Hunting!

DARRELL W. GURNEY, CPC
c/o HUNTER ARTS PUBLISHING
P.O. BOX 66578
LOS ANGELES, CA 90066
publisher@hunterarts.com

Resumes for Recruiters

This section will not attempt to cover the A-Z of resume creation. There are many resume preparation services and books detailing resume design on the market. However, here are some rules for *recruiter-preferred* resumes. Giving a headhunter what he wants in a resume increases your chances of being helped.

If you're sending a resume to a hiring company on your own, do what you like. If you're sending one to a recruiter, bells and whistles are specifically not needed. What is needed is a straight, simple, *chronological* resume. *Please, nothing fancy!* As a matter of fact, if a headhunter sees a resume that includes "creative elements," he immediately starts wondering what the person has to hide. A recruiter is concerned about skills and experience, not your artistic design—it scores no points. Also, because a headhunter needs to locate specific hiring criteria in your background quickly, she will not want to wade through a *functional* resume, where none of your experience can easily be traced to a job. In the search professional's mind, a functional resume is a red flag that the candidate is trying to cover up something: no marketable work experience, heavy job-hopping, employment gaps, etc. They work well for career *changers*, highlighting applicable experience that can be parlayed into other positions, but remember that a headhunter can generally only place you in a position similar to your past. So, a chronological resume, focusing specifically on the past, is what a recruiter wants.

Rather than illustrate the dos and don'ts of resume construction through scores of examples, I'll simply list them.

DON'T:

- Exceed 1-2 pages (unless you are a technical professional with a separate sheet of systems/software used).
- Cram a 3-page resume into 1 by shrinking margins and fonts—rewrite the resume to shorten.
- Use a "Functional" resume—too difficult to see what experience goes where.
- Use a book-fold, brochure-type resume—too long and cumbersome.
- Express your creative talents by using other-than-standard fonts, multiple columns, graphics, pictures, newspaper-like headlines, etc.—high database resistance and makes one wonder why you have to sell yourself so hard.
- State an objective—it's generally either so broad as to be useless or so narrow and specific as to cut you out of many opportunities. Communicate what you are looking for in the cover letter and let your experience speak for itself in the resume.
- Put "References Available Upon Request" at the bottom —everyone knows this.
- Put salary, employer addresses/phone numbers, or references on the resume—it takes up room and is unnecessary when being represented by a recruiter.

- Use paragraphs to explain job duties, experience, or accomplishments; rather, use bullet-points, capturing ideas in one short, concise line each.
- Use **Bold**, <u>underlines</u>, *italics*, ALL CAPS, or horizontal lines in the body text—creates database resistance.
- Use colored html backgrounds behind your e-mailed resume and cover letter—again, it appears that you have to sell yourself too hard. Look, we are recruiters: we're *going* to look at your resume to see if we can help you. You don't need to lure us.
- Isolate keywords out into a block—incorporate them into the resume contextually.

DO:

- Make your resume easy and inviting to read, with lots of white space.
- Use 1-inch margins on sides and at least ¾-inch on top and bottom.
- Use traditional, serif-type fonts (e.g., Times New Roman), not sans serif (e.g., Arial). Studies have shown that the little extra strokes and tails on the letters (compare the above) actually improve readability.
- Use the same font throughout the resume—don't mix fonts.
- Use a type size of 11- or 12-point, nothing smaller.
- Left-justify everything, to make transfer into the database easier.
- Use a "Chronological" resume—where all relevant experience and accomplishments obtained at each job are easily associated with that job, in descending order from most recent.
- State months *and* years of beginning and ending employment dates (in numbers, not words)—a recruiter will need to know anyhow, so you might as well put them in.

- State all education received, even if a degree was not completed—but don't make it look like you have a degree if you don't.
- Put all contact information on both the resume *and* the cover letter, including home, office, voice-mail, cellular, and pager numbers as well as private e-mail address.
- Fill up the entire page, separating ideas horizontally (not in vertical columns), with as much appropriate experience and as many keywords as possible.
- Put a short statement describing a company under its name if what they do is not evident.

5/95-8/00   **Monplanto Corporation**
(a $50B manufacturer of synthetic trees and shrubs)
Greenville, WI

Keywords

Where do you locate the keywords for your job or industry? Well, after reading this book, think like a headhunter—what words would one use to search a database for someone like you? A few ways to train yourself:

1. Look up classified job openings in the newspaper or online and see what employers in your field are asking for. Focus on the "want" of the want-ads.
2. After you've isolated those keywords that relate to your background, experience, skills, training, education, etc., compile them into groups of 4-6 words each and use these groups to search for resumes on Internet posting sites. If you find people like yourself, these words are good. If you don't, find better words.

With these basic guidelines established, let's critique the resumes presented in Part IV.

Maj. Lever Bose (Example 4.1, p. 119)

- Cover letter lacks full contact information but succinctly describes reasons for leaving, positions and industries of interest, salary and relocation preferences.
- Resume "Objective" basically says he wants to use his past experience in another job—unnecessary, and takes up room.
- Most "Accomplishments" are really job duties and responsibilities. Accomplishments should be something like "Project-managed a corporate-wide new technology migration 20% under budget and 4 weeks ahead of schedule." Accomplishments should be specific and measurable.
- Resume dates are spelled out or lack months. A consistent, simple format of "1/98-Present" or "4/96-1/98" takes up less space and conveys everything needed.
- Job duties, responsibilities, and experience are in paragraphs—hard to read and comprehend. Main ideas of each paragraph should be summarized in bullet-points of (preferably) one line each, whether in complete sentences or not. The first paragraph under Some Bank Credit Services would be more readable as:
  - Responsible for technology operations and implementations for high-volume call center with focus on financial/business impact.
  - Manage staff/projects in: Data Networking, Technology Integration, Quality, Desktop Applications, Telecommunications, Training & Development, Consultant Relationships, Help Desk, Communications and Facilities.
- He mentions the same keywords "Training and Development" twice in the first job, not to mention the entire resume. After ensuring he has it *once*, he should focus on other keywords.

- Major Lever Bose somewhat lives up to his name, using keywords redundantly at times. With a bit more effort, he could have groomed and tightened this resume to be shorter, rendering it more pleasing to the eye while maintaining its effectiveness.

Manny O. Namischen (Example 4.2, p. 131)

- As outlined in the chapter, narrow margins, with all caps and italics in places, make this a more difficult resume to OCR if it were faxed.
- The objective is only valuable in that it says he wants to remain in hi-tech—the rest is superfluous. "Objective: Hi-Tech Sales" is fine.
- No in-depth contact info. He *must* have at least a cell phone, if not a pager and e-mail address.
- Good use of bullet-points. Even with wider margins, this gives more space and readability to the resume.
- Good note of "President's Club," but strange to see no mention of "quotas" from a sales person.
- Good keywords relevant to the sales field except, of course, "sales" (duh!).
- Good employment dates.
- "References" statement unnecessary.
- Room to spare: could have elaborated more throughout the resume, loading it with more keywords and experience—unless he's shot his wad and this is all he has.

Pat Peeves (Example 4.3, p. 132)

- Good contact info, though a pager number might also be available.
- Good use of space, separating ideas horizontally rather than vertically.
- Good dates.
- Good bullet-points, with strong results stated.

- Good sales-related keywords, but left out some such as "business-to-business" or "canvassing."
- No objective is fine if she has spelled out her interests in a cover letter. Otherwise, an assumption would be made that she is interested in likewise "consultative" sales positions in related industries.
- "References" statement unnecessary.

Ima Goodun (Example 4.4, p. 140)

- Good contact info.
- An objective is fine in this case because it names specific titles, though it could be shorter.
- Summary O.K. to nail keywords that don't show up elsewhere, though the idea is to incorporate them into the text. At least she passes her keywords block off as a "Summary."
- Good keywords throughout.
- Good spelling out and abbreviation of SEC.
- Excellent overall resume.

Submitting Your E-mail Resume

In Chapter 4, I highly recommend e-mailed resume submission to today's recruiters. Here is a simple, step-by-step guide to cutting, pasting, and formatting an ASCII-text (pronounced "as-kee"-text) resume into the body of an e-mail along with an "attached" file version for nice, hardcopy purposes. Because it's so effortless for a headhunter to transfer the ASCII-text version into the database, submitting this way will cause the least "resistance" to your resume being included in relevant searches immediately. The attached file of the same resume in Word allows a recruiter to make a far nicer presentation of you to his client, given the ASCII-text version generally looks boring, plain, and often warped. Though many employers don't need the attached file if you submit to them directly, a headhunter definitely does.

The following steps can be used to create an e-mail submission to a recruiter from a resume constructed in Microsoft Word on a Windows system using Netscape Communicator as the e-mail browser. These basic steps, with slight alterations, can be used with other software or systems.

1. Open or create your resume in Word.
2. Set the right margin at 6½ inches.
3. Choose Select All from the Edit drop-down menu.
4. Choose Copy from the Edit drop-down menu.
5. Close out of Word after saving your work.
6. Two options here: a) go directly to your browser's e-mail messaging facility to paste the resume, or b) go to Notepad in the Accessories menu to tidy and prepare the resume before pasting it in the e-mail.
7. Enlarge the viewable screen to at least the size of your former Word version (6½ inches).
8. With your cursor in the body, choose Paste from the Edit drop-down menu of either Notepad or your e-mail message.
9. Nip and tuck the now ASCII-text version of your resume. Ideally use the word-wrap feature in the Edit drop-down menu (Notepad), or use "hard" carriage returns, to wrap word strings back that may be creeping outside of the margins. Also, replace any characters that did not convert from the Word version to ASCII-text (e.g., use asterisks or hyphens for bullet-points, etc.).
10. Add whatever introduction and cover letter you choose above the resume, adhering to the same margins. (You can cut and paste this in the same way you did the resume, but keep them together as one document.)
11. If you're in Notepad, now cut and paste this entire document into your e-mail messaging facility. (Open your browser's e-mail and select New Message.) Nip and tuck again if any word strings have gone astray or gaps/spaces have erupted.
12. Click Attach File in your browser.
13. Browse the hard drive to locate the original Word version of your resume and double-click it.

14. You now have a complete e-mail of your resume for submitting to a recruiter. It contains both an ASCII-text version and an attached file. E-mail yourself to check for any mistakes before sending it to the headhunter.

The only problem with e-mail is that, despite your best efforts to send an ASCII-text version with no unsightly word-wrap, depending on the recipient's browser, it may occur. However, sticking to these margins will nonetheless render your text version the most legible and "database-able." This process gives recruiters exactly what they need to immediately know if they can help you. If they can, it has you poised for timely database inclusion and/or client company presentation.

APPENDIX C

Resources

The Internet is constantly changing and expanding. It would be nearly impossible to list every recruiter-oriented resource it contains. Yet, this list of recruitment industry associations, networking organizations, and search-industry information providers can at least jump-start your connection with recruiters and their open positions:

The Alliance of Medical Recruiters (AMR)   http://www.physicianrecruiters.com
Over 75 healthcare recruitment firms nationwide make up AMR, a recruiters association which supports the sharing of client and candidate resources among members.

All-Star Employment Network   http://www.allstarnetwork.com
New affiliation of recruiters serving a wide array of specialties. The site is currently geared toward obtaining members but may provide access to affiliate job openings in the future.

The American Association of Finance and Accounting (AAFA)   http://www.aafa.com
250 high-caliber search firms specializing in the fields of Finance and Accounting. Focused on CPA and MBA professionals, member firms network (make split placements) with one another, so plugging into one can connect you with many.

The Association of Executive Search Consultants (AESC)   http://www.aesc.org
Composed of 160 member firms worldwide, this is a professional association of exclusively retained-search organizations. More a trade association and less a networking organization,

AESC exists mainly to promote public awareness of the executive search business and to enhance industry professionalism.

Christian Recruiters   http://www.christianrecruiters.com

Small but proud association of Christian recruiters focusing specifically on the healthcare industry. Promotes networking among members.

Exec-U-Net   http://www.execunet.com

A membership service for executives. This year over 4,500 search firms and companies will post over 20,000 senior executive-level positions with Exec-U-Net. Over 70% of executive members are currently employed; over 75% have salaries greater than $100,000, 25% with salaries greater than $200,000; over 67% have advanced degrees.

First Interview   http://www.firstinterview.net

A professional association of 250 search firms focusing specifically in the fields of Sales and Marketing. Promotes heavy networking among members.

Kennedy Information, Inc.   http://www.kennedyinfo.com

Yearly publisher of *The Directory of Executive Recruiters*, also known as the "Red Book." Available in bookstores and libraries (careers or reference section), you can also conduct a headhunter search online. Site lists various other books and resources.

National Association of Executive Recruiters (NAER)   http://www.naer.org

Founded in 1984, NAER membership is a "seal of approval," stating that a firm upholds the standards upon which the association is based. Does not necessarily promote networking.

National Association of Personnel Services (NAPS)   http://www.napsweb.org

The oldest trade association of the staffing industry, NAPS represents over 1800 firms across the country and administers the only industry professional certification, the Certified Personnel Consultant (CPC) designation. Member recruiters are segmented online by areas of specialty and geography.

National Banking Network (NBN)   http://www.nbn-jobs.com

The oldest and largest networking association of independently-owned recruiting firms specializing in the Banking and Financial Services fields.

National Personnel Associates (NPA)   http://www.npainc.com

The oldest professional association of executive search firms with over 400 affiliates in the U.S. and overseas. Firms focus on a variety of specialties including Sales, Human Resources, Finance, Engineering, High-tech/MIS/IT, Healthcare, Executive Management, etc. Promotes heavy networking among members.

NETSHARE   http://www.netshare.com

A membership service for executives. Currently assists more than 2,300 executive subscribers and receives position listings from nearly 7000 search consultants worldwide. Maintains more than 1,400 job postings, validated and updated daily. Selected by FORTUNE magazine as a "best search site for executives."

Net-Temps   http://www.net-temps.com

Founded in 1994, Net-Temps boasts a cross-posting distribution of classified employment ads to over 500 Internet search engines, portals, directories, on-line services, and newsgroups. Though permanent job seekers will also benefit, as the name implies, the focus is on professionals seeking temporary or contract work through recruitment firms.

Private Source   http://www.private-source.com

Newly launched, this site provides access to a nationwide directory of executive recruiters and their open positions. Offers a notification service (they will call you!) when a recruiter expresses interest in your confidentially "coded" background.

Recruiters Alliance   http://www.recruitersalliance.com

A professional online network of retained, contingency, contract and temporary staffing agencies worldwide. Job seekers can have their resume e-mailed directly to member recruiters.

Recruiters Online Network (RON)   http://www.recruitersonline.com

Over 8,000 registered recruiters make RON the world's largest association of recruiters, executive search firms, employment agencies, and headhunters. Used by members as a posting venue for searches and an avenue for split placements.

The Search Bulletin   http://www.searchbulletin.com

A membership service for executives. This career tool boasts that almost one-third of the subscribers who report landing a new position attribute their success to the Bulletin. Four of the nation's top 10 graduate business schools have chosen The Search Bulletin as the best career management information service for their alumni.

SearchNet International   http://www.searchnetint.com

Operating in all five continents, SearchNet provides access to top executive recruiters specializing in high-level, international management positions.

Top Echelon   http://www.topechelon.com

A worldwide network of over 2,500 affiliated recruiters. Members place over 32,000 people annually and completed over 5,000 split placements in the past 4 years.

The following sites will provide access to positions being filled by recruiters as well as other professional job-search services. This list is in no way exhaustive—but hopefully still accurate:

AccountantJobs   http://www.accountantjobs.com

Site specifically focused on all levels of the accounting profession.

America's Job Bank   http://www.ajb.dni.us

A partnership between the US Department of Labor and the state employment services. Literally lists over a million jobs ranging from professional and technical to blue collar, from management and sales to clerical.

American Jobs   http://www.americanjobs.com

Specifically geared toward hi-tech computer and engineering jobs, its database is queried over 2 million times per month. Job postings are updated hourly.

CareerBuilder Network   http://www.careerbuilder.com

CareerBuilder's "Mega Job Search" technology provides access to nearly every job on the Internet by combining over 25 leading career Web sites. Offers a Personal Search Agent for notification of interesting opportunities.

CareerCentral   http://www.careercentral.com

A more private online matchmaking service connecting professionals with pre-screened opportunities and employers with pre-screened professionals.

CareerCity   http://www.careercity.com

From the publisher of the *JobBank* and *Knock'em Dead* books, CareerCity has won numerous awards and serves over 2.5 million page views per month.

CareerMart   http://www.careermart.com

Partnered with some of the Internet's heaviest traveled Web sites, CareerMart is a popular "click-through" for job seekers.

Career Mosaic   http://www.careermosaic.com

Offers job search by specialty among thousands of positions and big-name employers, Online Job Fairs, a Career Resource Center, and even free e-mail.

CareerPark   http://www.careerpark.com

View job listings by category or employer. Also has a Resource Center to connect you with other job-posting and professional services.

CareerPath   http://www.careerpath.com

Co-founded in 1995, CareerPath is owned by eight major newspapers and boasts the "freshest" jobs anywhere, with no position remaining on the database for more than two weeks.

CareerSite   http://www.careersite.com

Uses advanced technology to connect job seekers, employers, and intermediaries. Has registered over 200,000 job seekers in its database.

Careers Wall Street Journal   http://www.careers.wsj.com

More career services, support, and listings than you can handle in one log-on session.

Classifieds 2000   http://www.classifieds2000.com

A division of the popular Excite search engine. Click on the Employment tab on the home page (or buy a car and find a roommate).

C/net's Search
http://www.search.com

Search job postings in more than 100 newsgroups worldwide with one mouse click. Lists various other online job search resources.

Dice
http://www.dice.com

A 10-year old (a long time in Internet years!) service focusing on the IT industry. Programmers, software engineers, systems administrators, and systems analysts can have their immediate availability for permanent and contract positions "announced" to all member recruiters.

Environmental Career Center
http://www.ecconet.com

Site specifically focused on Environmental, Health, and Safety professionals.

ExecutivesOnly
http://www.executivesonly.com

As the name implies, this site focuses on professionals with an annual earning potential of $70K-750K and lists only positions in that range.

GetJobs
http://www.getjobs.com

A multi-specialty job and resume posting service.

Headhunter
http://www.headhunter.net

On average, 100,000 users visit Headhunter.net every day. The site now has over 150,000 current job listings, with salary ranges from entry-level to over $500,000. The top 5 specialties represented are Information Technology, Engineering, Accounting, Sales and Marketing. Hosts CareerBYTES, a newsletter for job seekers.

JobEngine
http://www.jobengine.com

Ziff-Davis Publications' Internet arm, ZDNet, is partnered with I-Search to provide a matchmaking site for computer industry employers and professionals.

JobOptions
http://www.joboptions.com

One of the pioneers in online employment recruiting, JobOptions was originally known as AdNet and then E.span. Hosts job and resume posting/distribution and career-related content.

Jobs   http://www.jobs.com
The largest locally focused employment site, Jobs.com has local career hubs in 19 major cities and 77 other metro centers. Also offers its "Resumail" service, which takes certain glitches out of the resume distribution process.

Jobs & Adverts (USA)   http://www.jausa.com
The US subsidiary of one of Europe's leading Internet-based job posting services. With locations in Bangkok, Vienna, Zurich, Frankfurt, and Washington, D.C., this site can connect you with many international opportunities.

JobStar   http://www.jobstar.org
Primarily focused on the California employment market, former JobSmart has changed its name to JobStar. This is a more career-guidance oriented site, praised by career-guidance guru Richard Nelson Bolles.

JobTrak   http://www.jobtrak.com
Partnered with over 900 college career centers nationwide. Focuses on listings for graduates and alumni.

Monster   http://www.monster.com
The new combined site for merged online job-listing mammoths Monster Board and Online Career Center. Posting over 210,000 job opportunities, there's something for everyone. Also provides advice in the Career Zones section.

NationalJobBank   http://www.nationaljobbank.com
Hosts and links to sites of various search firms with available positions. For a small fee, resumes can be posted for 6 months with a direct e-mail link to you.

NationJob Network   http://www.nationjob.com
Receives approximately 4 million hits per week; offers P.J. Scout, a private search agent that notifies the job seeker of appropriate opportunities.

Passport Access   http://www.passportaccess.com
Job and resume posting site specifically geared toward the technical fields.

PlanetRecruit   http://www.planetrecruit.com

International in scope, as the name implies, this site lists positions in over 80 countries. Originally focused on Information Technology positions, PlanetRecruit now supports a wide array of fields.

PursuitNet   http://www.pursuit.com

Originally organized to provide job posting and search for the software and hi-tech management consulting fields, PursuitNet has branched into the telecommunications, aerospace, financial, and sales/marketing arenas.

RecruitUSA   http://www.recruitusa.com

Hosts a database updated daily with the most current career opportunities on the Internet. Allows for localized search through state newsgroups and government resources.

6FigureJobs   http://www.6figurejobs.com

The name says it all: only posts career opportunities with guaranteed compensation packages of more than $100,000. The only executive-level site singled out in *U.S. News and World Report*'s "Best of the Web" awards.

Vault Reports   http://www.vaultreports.com

A full-on career management site, with job postings, specific industry research, message boards, and a "career store."

The Works USA   http://www.theworksusa.com

A window to several job and resume posting sites, each geared to a particular job seeker: SalesWorks, FinancialWorks, MedicalWorks, LegalWorks, InfoWorks (computer jobs), and CollegeWorks.

Weddle's Web Guide   http://www.weddles.com

Recommended by *Fortune* Magazine, Weddle's is a total job seeker's Internet resource. Offers books, newsletters, and Internet advice to assist all participants in the job search and hiring process.

Yahoo!   http://www.yahoo.com

Yahoo! Need I say more? Hosts online career advice by headhunter/author Nick Corcodilos. Click on "Jobs" under the Business & Economy heading, then "Recruiting and Placement."

And if all that ain't enough to boggle your career mind, here are a few search engines/directories that can point you to further recruiter resources:

Alta Vista http://www.altavista.com

Alta Vista search engine's posting and career site. Click on "Jobs" under the Business & Finance heading, then "Executive Search."

HotBot http://www.hotbot.com

Click on the Recruiters category in this "most award-winning search engine." Click on "Jobs," then "Executive Search."

100Hot http://www.100hot.com/directory/business/jobs.html

Lists the 100 most popular job sites, most of which list recruiter's openings.

Infoseek http://infoseek.go.com/Center/Careers/Jobs

Both a posting site hosted by CareerPath as well as a directory of other career-oriented services.

Lycos http://dir.lycos.com/Business/Jobs

Click on the Recruiters category.

Glossary of Terms

attached file: an added file (Word version of a resume) included with an e-mail

ASCII-text: American Standard Code for Information Interchange, this comprises the character sets used in almost all present-day computers; pronounced "as-kee," it is the most basic form of text document

bargain shop: a recruiting firm charging lower than standard fees (often reflected in service)

bird-dogging: a headhunter's process of asking for candidate or client referrals

"blasting" service: an Internet resource contracting with you to promulgate your resume to recruiters or companies, sometimes indiscriminately and usually impersonally; may not always include both the text *and* attachment of your resume

buffering: the recruiter's activity as intermediary between candidate and company in the placement and new hire periods

buzzwords: words or phrases specific to a particular job or industry; highly keyword searchable

candidate: a job-seeker being assisted by a headhunter or considered for employment by a hiring company

candidate-driven market: when there are more jobs available than there are qualified professionals to fill them; often associated with a strong economy, it is also related to the size of the workforce; this market puts more power in the hands of the job-seeker

career equity: the working professional's equivalent of "owner's equity;" the value of one's career enhanced by obtaining the highest return from one's employable assets

career partner: a headhunter operating as a candidate's lifetime personal manager, of sorts, with information and opportunities to help them best achieve career goals

chronological resume: resume style focused on the chronological detailing of specific functions, duties, and accomplishments related to each employer; preferred by recruiters

coding: a process used with early recruiting databases whereby all candidate information was categorized into codes for information storage and retrieval

container: a hybrid of contingency and retained search, possessing elements of each; an agreement whereby a company pays a certain portion of recruiter's fee up-front which helps the recruiter "contain" the client—elicit a commitment from them—thereby reducing the risk associated with straight contingency work

contingency: basis of search firm operation whereby a headhunter is paid *contingent* upon the client hiring their candidate; fee is paid *after* placement is made

CPC (Certified Personnel Consultant):   akin to a CPA, a professional designation conferred upon recruiters based upon rigorous testing, experience, and continuing education

CSAM (Certified Senior Account Manager):   a professional designation used specifically within the firm of Management Recruiters International (MRI) to recognize top consultants meeting certain educational and effectiveness requirements

database resistance: the dynamic of a database *resisting* the inclusion of a resume based on the time, labor, and attention required to translate it into KWS database form; the more amenable the original form, the lower the resistance

emergency career management: a last minute search process, when one needs a job immediately

employable assets: those personal and professional skills, qualities, and attributes which make a candidate uniquely valuable in the marketplace

employer-driven market: when there are more qualified professionals available than there are positions for them to fill;

often associated with a weak economy; this market puts more power in the hands of the hiring company

fall off: when a placed candidate leaves or is terminated by an employer before the completion of the guarantee period; means either a need to replace the candidate or no fee for the recruiter

flesh-peddler: derogatory term for a recruiter who simply throws bodies around without focusing on client or candidate service

functional resume: resume style focused on functions or capabilities, not associated with any particular job, and only briefly listing employers; *not* preferred by recruiters

going around: using client or candidate information obtained from a headhunter to either obtain employment or an employee without compensating the headhunter

guarantee period: akin to a manufacturers warranty, a trial period in which it becomes clear that a placed candidate and job are a "match;" if a placed candidate leaves a company within this time frame (quitting, being terminated), the recruiter's fee is lowered or eliminated

headhunters: messengers of opportunity; also known as "professional recruiters" or "search consultants"

hidden job market: those openings worked by search professionals not always advertised elsewhere by client companies

KWS (keyword searchable) database: the memory of a contemporary search firm, this computerized "filing" system allows any resume to be retrieved by searching for specific words or phrases

loading: cramming a resume or cover letter with specific keywords or phrases related to employment background, skills, or aspirations

marginal candidate: job-seeker a headhunter judges not strongly marketable

marketable candidate: job-seeker a headhunter judges highly placeable

NAPS (National Association of Personnel Services): the oldest professional association of recruiters; administers the CPC (Certified Personnel Consultant) program

networks: associated recruiters with whom headhunters split placements (one providing the candidate, the other the client)

OCR (Optical Character Recognition): a process whereby software translates the markings on an image (resume) into letters and words of text through an internal vocabulary system

optimal employment: job in which the value of employable assets are maximized, netting the highest return for the employee (money, growth, location, etc.)

out-source: an HR department's need to delegate a function (recruiting/hiring) to outside providers (headhunters)

paper-pusher: derogatory term for a recruiter who simply throws resumes around without focusing on client or candidate service

placement: when a candidate begins work for a headhunter's client

Recruiter's Pipeline: the funnel system through which the individual channels of searches, Candidates, and Send Outs result in Placements—and perfect jobs

resume: that document which spells out (preferably chronologically) a professional's employment experience, contact information, and all worthy KWS criteria; should be updated regularly, especially after starting a new position

retained: basis of search firm operation whereby a headhunter is paid up-front, *before* the placement is made

retrievable: a document (resume) able to be located within a database

ROA (Return on Ability): akin to a company owner's ROI (Return on Investment); the payoff that a working professional receives from his investment of ability

ROE (Return on Effort): akin to a company owner's ROI (Return on Investment); the payoff that a working professional receives from her investment of effort

rubber resumes: characterized by heavy job-hopping

scanners: peripherals which effectively "photograph" a resume for computer digitizing

searches: positions a headhunter works to fill for client companies

search firm: an enterprise focused on isolating, recruiting, and placing specific employees for hiring employers

seeing beyond the paper: the ability to perceive and/or explore a job-seeker's value beyond what is spelled out in a resume

send out: arranged interview between a headhunter's candidate and client

Send Out/Placement Ratio: the statistic showing the relative effectiveness of a recruiter in turning send outs into placements

spam: the indiscriminate and impersonal dissemination of materials such as resumes

specialties: the fields in which headhunters confine their activities, whether by occupations (Sales, Finance, etc.) or industries (Hi-Tech, Pharmaceutical, etc.).

split fees: the "halving" of placement fees by networking recruiters

systems: recruiter's computerized and other support mechanisms aiding their job performance

text file: the basic form of computerized information including simple text; unlike a word-processed file, a text file includes no "bells and whistles" such as bold text, bullet-points, etc

wish list: that document which spells out a professional's criteria for desired job opportunities; should be updated regularly, especially after starting a new position

WO/WI (Words In/Words Out) factor: a recruiter's speaking/listening ratio; should be less than 1 in a new headhunter relationship

INDEX

About the Author

Darrell W. Gurney, Certified Personnel Consultant (CPC), has been a professional recruiter for over 14 years. A Summa Cum Laude graduate of the University of Texas with degrees in Finance and International Business, he spent his early career with Arthur Young (Ernst & Young) and MGM/United Artists Pictures. Based in Los Angeles, his search firm places professionals worldwide through affiliation with over 600 executive recruiters. Microsoft, America Online, Hunt-Wesson, and American Express have all utilized Darrell's professional services, just to name a few. He writes and lectures on search industry issues.

Order Form

FAX ORDERS:	(310) 821-6308. Send this form.
TELEPHONE ORDERS	Call 1 (877) 4HEADHUNT toll free,
	(443-2348). Have your credit card ready.
ONLINE ORDERS:	http://www.hunterarts.com.
POSTAL ORDERS:	Hunter Arts Publishing,
	P.O. Box 66578B, Los Angeles, CA 90066
	USA, (310) 821-6303

Please send _____ copies of
HEADHUNTERS *Revealed!*
Career Secrets for Choosing and Using Professional Recruiters
at $14.95 each.

I understand that I may return any book
for a full refund if not satisfied.

Please add **$4** for the first book and **$2** for each additional book for shipping in the US. Internationally, add **$9** for the first book and **$5** for each additional book.
Please add **8.25%** for each book shipped to California addresses ($1.24 per book).

❑ Please inform me of the speaking and consulting services offered by Darrell W. Gurney, CPC.

Name: _____

Address: _____

_____

City: _____ State: _____ Zip: _____

Telephone: _____

E-mail address: _____

Payment: ❑ Check   Credit Card: ❑ Visa ❑ MasterCard

Card number: _____

Name on Card: _____ Exp. Date: _____